PRACTICAL SCIENCE

TEACHING WITHIN THE
NATIONAL CURRICULUM

GRAEME KENT

I am grateful to the staff and children of St Thomas' Primary School, Boston, Lincs., for all their help in the preparation of this book. I would particularly like to thank my friends and colleagues Mrs Kathleen Pearson and Mrs Ruth Bishop for preparing the list of suggestions for science projects.

Published by Scholastic Publications Ltd,
Villiers House, Clarendon Avenue,
Leamington Spa, Warwickshire CV32 5PR.

© 1990 Scholastic Publications Ltd
Reprinted 1991

Written by Graeme Kent
Edited by Anne Faundez
Sub-edited by Catherine Baker
Designed by Sue Limb
Illustrated by Martin Aitchison
Photographs by:
John Birdsall, p39
Bob Bray, pp9, 40, 145, 153
RJ Davis, p127
Brian Gadsby, p52
Chris Kelly, p71
Jane Miller Collection, p136
Brian Mould, p140
Robert A Smith, p44
John Twinning, pp5, 57
Terry Williams, p48
Every effort has been made to trace the
photographers whose work has been used
in this book, and the publishers apologise
for any inadvertent omissions.

Typeset by Studio Photoset, Leicester
Artwork by Norfolk House Graphic
Designers Ltd., Leicester
Printed by Ebenezer Baylis, Worcester

Front cover artwork by David Sim
Front cover designed by Joy White

British Library Cataloguing in Publication Data
Kent, Graeme 1933-
A practical guide to teaching science within the national
curriculum.
1. Great Britain. Primary schools. Curriculum subjects:
Science. Teaching
I. Title
372.350440941

ISBN 0-590-76018-1

Contents

Appendices   169

Other Scholastic books   174

Introduction

Science in the National Curriculum

Reservations have been expressed by primary school teachers about the implications of science in the National Curriculum. How, they ask, is it going to be put into practice with Class 4 on a wet Friday afternoon? That will continue to be the responsibility of the individual teacher. The guidelines do not attempt to be prescriptive about how science is to be taught, or about the amount of time to be devoted to it.

It is the *content* of the curriculum which must be delivered, and that is laid down in the key stages and attainment targets. For some, this may present a problem; but for many it will be a relief.

Science has always occupied a tenuous position in primary schools. In many it has hardly been taught at all. The position was summed up in the 1978 report *Primary Education in England* (HMSO):

'Few primary schools visited in the course of this survey had effective programmes for the teaching of science. There was lack of appropriate equipment; insufficient attention was given to ensuring proper coverage of key scientific notions; the teaching of processes and skills such as observing, the formulating of hypotheses, experimenting and recording was often superficial. The work in observational and experimental science was less well matched to children's capabilities than work in any other area of the curriculum.'

The guidelines which have been set down in the National Curriculum have now given us the foundations upon which we can develop a science curriculum as part of the overall educational provision for children in our schools. How we can build this curriculum is the subject of this book.

What is science?

The purpose of science in the primary school is to enable children to understand the world in which they live by showing them how to investigate it in a systematic fashion.

In order to do this, most teachers will try to make use of children's natural curiosity about their surroundings. Drawing on this curiosity, a teacher can show children how to observe, study, question, plan, investigate and experiment, relate findings, draw conclusions, understand and record how things are – and also the ways in which things sometimes change.

The first responsibility of the teacher is to use the National Curriculum guidelines to draw up a scheme of work, or a detailed teaching plan. In order to do so, it would be advisable for teachers to think carefully about the following questions:
● Which areas of science should be covered? (Aims.)
● What should the child understand? (Concepts.)
● What should the child feel? (Attitudes.)
● What should the child be able to do? (Skills.)
● What should the child know? (Knowledge.)

Attainment targets

There are now five revised attainment targets in the National Curriculum for Science. Attainment Target 1, Scientific investigation, can be assimilated into the other ATs and does not necessarily have to be addressed entirely on its own.

The National Curriculum for science in the primary school is divided into two key stages. Broadly speaking, Key Stage 1 covers years 1 and 2 in the Infants. Key Stage 2 deals with years 3, 4, 5 and 6 in the Juniors.

Subject- or project-based?

A scheme of work could deal with the science curriculum by covering each attainment target in turn, but this will be difficult to achieve considering the constraints on time. It will generally prove more effective if the attainment targets are included progressively in a number of projects spread over the school year. These projects could be part of a cross-curricular base for the whole curriculum.

Exploration of science

Attainment Target 1, Scientific investigation suggests some of the ways in which science should be approached in the primary school. This attainment target need not be tackled on its own but could be an integral part of the scheme of work. Attainment Target 1 emphasises the need to:
● Involve the children in considering ideas and looking for solutions.
● Encourage the children to explore objects and events at first hand.
● Help the children to use non-standard measures like hand-spans, and to make use of simple measuring skills.
● Make sure the children are aware of the need for care and safety at all times.
● Give the children opportunities to sort, group and describe objects, using their senses and marking similarities and differences.
● Develop the skills of systematic recording of results, using a wide variety of appropriate methods.
● Encourage the interpretation of results.
● Help the children to report orally and in writing and by any other relevant methods.

How to use this book

The book is divided into two main sections: Key Stage 1 for Infants and Key Stage 2 for Juniors.

In the National Curriculum there is some overlapping. In Key Stage 1, the children are asked to cover Levels 1 to 3; while in Key Stage 2 they are asked to cover Levels 2 to 5. To prevent duplication in this book, Key Stage 1 deals with Levels 1 and 2, while Key Stage 2 covers Levels 3 to 5. If a teacher using Key Stage 1 finds that the children need more material, then she merely has to adapt some of the Level 3 activities from Key Stage 2 which are to be found later in the book.

In chapters One and Four, which deal with delivering the attainment targets in Key Stages 1 and 2 respectively, each attainment target in turn is discussed and a number of relevant scientific activities are given. These are dealt with progressively, starting with Level 1 in Key Stage 1 and going on to Level 2. In Key Stage 2, the activities for each attainment target start at Level 3 and go on to Level 5.

Chapters One and Four consider each of the attainment targets individually, but divide them further, using the original attainment target names to qualify them. Thus, the original attainment target names appear in brackets after the new titles.

It is suggested that the teacher include a number of attainment targets in any one project, perhaps using the table on page 8 for reference, and including the activities suggested here for each relevant attainment target, together with others of her own composition. There are suggestions in the text for dividing the attainment targets into projects, and also for including these projects in cross-curricular activities.

A progressive topic list to cover the science curriculum

	Year 1	Year 2	Year 3	Year 4	Year 5	Year 6
Autumn term	Harvest (ATs 1, 2, 3, 5)	Myself (ATs 1, 2, 3, 4, 5)	Transport (ATs 1, 4, 5)	Change (ATs 1, 2, 3, 5)	Food (ATs 1, 2, 3, 4, 5)	Solar system (ATs 1, 2, 3, 4, 5)
	Toys (ATs 1, 4, 5)	Hot and cold (ATs 1, 2, 3, 4, 5)	Music (ATs 1, 4, 5)	Night and day (ATs 1, 2, 3)	Health (ATs 1, 2, 3, 5)	Ecology (ATs 1, 2, 3, 4, 5)
Spring term	Time (ATs 1, 2, 3)	Weather (ATs 1, 2, 3, 5)	Homes (ATs 1, 2, 3, 5)	The Earth (ATs 1, 2, 3, 4, 5)	Colours (ATs 1, 2, 3, 4, 5)	Islands (ATs 1, 2, 3)
	Sound (ATs 1, 5)	Animals of long ago (ATs 1, 2, 3, 4)	Movement (ATs 1, 2, 3, 5)	Farming (ATs 1, 2, 3, 4, 5)	Clothes (ATs 1, 2, 3, 4)	Beginnings of life (ATs 1, 2, 3, 5)
Summer term	Growth (ATs 1, 2, 3, 5)	Our school (ATs 1, 2, 3, 4, 5)	Waste (ATs 1, 2, 3, 4)	Sound (ATs 1, 2, 4, 5)	Holidays (ATs 1, 2, 3)	Pollution (ATs 1, 2, 3, 4, 5)
	Creatures around us (ATs 1, 2, 3)	Water (ATs 1, 2, 3, 5)	The play park (ATs 1, 2, 3, 4, 5)	Markets (ATs 1, 2, 3, 4)	Air (ATs 1, 2, 3, 4)	Buildings (ATs 1, 3, 4)

These projects could be used either one for every half term or, in a school with vertically grouped children, one every term on a two-year cycle to prevent children repeating a topic.

Chapter One
Delivering the attainment targets

The original attainment targets for science were:

AT1: Exploration of science
AT2: The variety of life
AT3: Processes of life
AT4: Genetics and evolution
AT5: Human influences on the Earth
AT6: Types and uses of materials
AT7: Making new materials
AT8: Explaining how materials behave
AT9: Earth and atmosphere
AT10: Forces
AT11: Electricity and magnetism
AT12: The scientific aspects of information technology including microelectronics
AT13: Energy
AT14: Sound and music
AT15: Using light and electromagnetic radiation
AT16: The Earth in space
AT17: The nature of science

In 1991 these were condensed to give the following five attainment targets:

AT1: Scientific investigation
AT2: Life and living processes
AT3: Earth and environment
AT4: Materials and their behaviour
AT5: Energy and its effects.

Even the most apathetic or timid infant should enjoy some aspect of observing wildlife at first hand. Initially, her interest may be confined to staring at worms in a vivarium, feeding goldfish in a bowl or planting mustard seeds. Her curiosity could then be built upon to include a more general investigation of animals and plants, using books, television programmes and videos. From a simple but wide-ranging survey of the habitat, movement and nutrition of different sorts of wildlife, the child could then be encouraged to embark upon a practical course of looking after and beginning to understand a variety of living things in the school.

Level 1

To enable them to grasp the concept that there is a great diversity of living things, children should be given plenty of chances to examine various types of wildlife in the school and playground and to observe their similarities and differences. Living things can be recorded and listed according to the ways in which they move, their size and their shape. The children can then draw some of the creatures they have observed, and write and talk about them.

Animals can be studied to find out what they do in different types of weather, and the reactions of plants to rain, frost, snow and wind can also be examined and recorded. Young children should always be encouraged to put forward possible reasons for what they have seen.

Children can compare the pictures on seed packets with the real thing, assessing the differences and similarities between the pictures and the plants which come from the seeds. In order to understand the need of plants for certain specific conditions in which to live, children should have an opportunity to study plants' growth at first hand.

Level 2

Water and growth
What you need
Mustard seeds, blotting paper, water, jars, onions.

What to do
The importance of water for growth can be studied by putting some mustard seeds on a piece of damp blotting paper, and some on dry blotting paper. Which seeds grow? Can the children give a possible reason for this?

● Fill a jar with water, and place an onion in the neck of the jar so that it touches the water. Place another onion in the neck of a jar with no water in it. After a few days, compare the two onions. Which has grown? What could be the reason for this?

Sunlight and growth
What you need
Two identical pot plants, water, pencils, paper.

What to do
Obtain two identical pot plants. Water them both regularly, but place one in the sunlight and the other in a dark corner. After a few weeks, ask the children to compare, discuss and record the rates of growth and to give reasons for any disparities.

Ask the children to identify light and dark areas in a field or garden and to observe how the growth of plants is affected depending on where they are situated. Encourage them to compare dry and moist soils, and decide which sort seems to offer the best growing conditions for seeds.

Caring for living things
What you need
Snails, wooden box, dry soil, stones, caterpillar, fresh leaves, jar, water, plastic sheeting.

What to do
There are plenty of ways in which children can be shown that living things need to be treated with care and consideration. Many of these involve rearing creatures in the classroom.

Put some snails in a wooden box and cover the bottom of the box with dry soil and a few stones. Cover the top with plastic sheeting loosely tacked down so the snails can breathe. Put in plenty of green food for the snails, and change it daily.
● Bring a caterpillar into the classroom on the leaf upon which you found it. Cut a supply of similar leaves still on the stem. Put some soil in the bottom of a glass jar and place the leaves and caterpillar inside. Keep the stems fresh by placing them in a pot of water inside the jar. What changes occur in the caterpillar over a period of time?

Information technology

● Study the different ways in which birds and animals communicate with one another.
● Make a list of the noises made by different creatures.
● Listen to recordings of many different animal noises and observe the creatures on television.
● Use these activities to examine the different ways in which people communicate, for example by talking, writing, signalling and gesticulating.

Cross-curricular activities

● Allow the children to read the following story books, or read them to the class: *Puppy in the Park* by Helen Piers (Methuen); *The Very Hungry Caterpillar* by Eric Carle (Hamish Hamilton/Puffin) and *Millions of Cats* by Wanda Gag (Faber and Faber/Puffin).
● Encourage the children to construct a model caterpillar made from a strip of a large egg-box and paint it green.
● Let the children make a simple map showing the main distribution of wildlife in the area of the school. Link this with activities in geography.

Summary

● The children should understand the concept that all things may be divided into the categories of living, dead and non-living. They should also begin to appreciate that there are many different kinds of living things, all of which should be treated with consideration and concern, and all of which have their own particular needs.
● The children should develop the skills of sorting and grouping objects according to various categories, and they should also have experience with looking after pets and plants in the classroom, and studying the environment.
● Among the basic facts which children should learn at this stage are the following. Plants grow and stay in one place. Animals can be divided into many different groups, including mammals, birds, fish and insects. All mammals have hair and their young feed on their mothers' milk. All birds have two wings and two feet, and they all have feathers, but they do not all fly. Insects have six legs. Fish have gills to help them breathe in the water and fins which help them to swim.

AT2: Life and living processes – B
(Processes of life)

Help children to understand that both creatures and plants can be divided into different parts; that each part has its own functions; that living things reproduce their own kind; and that it is important to keep well and healthy.

Level 1

Help the children realise that some objects are living and others non-living, by taking them round the school and showing them a number of objects. Ask them to categorise each one as living or non-living after they have answered questions about the objects. Does it grow? Does it have young or reproduce in any way? Does it take in food? Does it give off waste? If the answers to most of these questions are *yes*, then the object is living.

The children could be asked to place these items into lists of 'Things which are alive' and 'Things which have never lived'.

Parts of the body and parts of plants

What you need

Pictures of the human body and of plants, pencils.

What to do

To familiarise the children with the external parts of the human body every opportunity should be taken to enable them to use parts of their bodies. They could be asked a number of questions about their bodies: What can our arms be used for? What can we do with our legs? Which parts of our bodies do we use when we crawl? How can we move our heads?

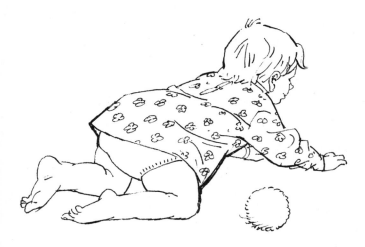

● Distribute copies of a simple picture showing the outline of the human body to the children and ask them to label as many parts as they can.
● Repeat this process using a simple outline of a plant. How many parts of the plant can each child name?

Level 2

There are a number of activities in which the children can participate in order to understand that living things reproduce their own kind.

Living things reproduce

What you need

Potato, flower-pot, box, soil, sand, plastic sheeting, photographs of the children in the class.

What to do

Place a potato in a dark box with a hole to admit air. It will soon produce white roots.

Half fill a flower-pot with soil and a little sand and plant the potato. Water the pot and cover it with plastic sheeting. Keep the pot full of soil, so that the potato does not appear.

After a few weeks, empty the pot and ask the children to discuss what they see.
● Help the children to make a study of babies. Ask them to bring to school photographs of themselves soon after they were born. Then they can try to guess which photographs represent which children.

Invite a mother with her baby to the classroom to talk to the children about how the baby is looked after and the course of its day.
● These activities could be linked with a general survey of how mammals look after their young. Use television programmes, films and books to provide background material for the project.

Keeping clean

What you need

Soap, water, oil, jar.

What to do

Explain the importance of soap and water in keeping clean. Show that water alone is not enough for personal cleanliness and that soap is also needed. Collect as many different kinds of soap as possible. Use them on stains and decide which is the most effective.

- Show how soap can clean stains by placing some oil in a jar of water. When the oil floats to the surface, put some soap in the water. Ask the children to describe what the soap does to the oil. Compare the speed and effectiveness of different soaps in dispersing the oil.
- Take every opportunity to stress the importance of hygiene in the handling of food and of washing hands after using the toilet and so on.
- Link these activities with work on the importance of eating and sleeping property.

Pattern of the day

The children should be encouraged to study the patterns of their own days as a springboard to studying the life patterns of animals and the main stages in human growth – childhood, adolescence, adulthood and old age.

What you need
Pencils, paper.

What to do
Ask each child to fill in the pattern of a typical day by talking about or writing down what she has eaten for each meal or snack. Use this activity as the basis for a series of comparisons leading to the compilation of wall-charts on subjects such as 'Our favourite breakfasts' and 'Our favourite lunches'. Follow up with work on nutrition.

Information technology

- In a study of the importance of our senses of sight, hearing, touch, taste and smell, look at technological aids for the deaf and the blind: radio, specially devised television programmes and talking books.

Cross-curricular activities

- In a study of the functions of parts of the body, read to the children *The Iron Man* by Ted Hughes (Faber and Faber), especially the passage in which the Iron Man starts putting himself together again after his fall over the cliff edge.
- Use activities on the reproduction of plants as the initial stage of a school sex-education policy.
- Use a number of hard-boiled eggs to explain about the reproduction of birds. Then let the children turn the eggs into chicks by attaching coloured pieces of felt to the eggs to represent beaks and feet and drawing in some eyes with coloured pens.

Summary

- In order to keep healthy we need to take exercise and eat and drink sensibly. We also need rest, and should keep ourselves clean.
- The children should have some knowledge of the exterior parts of the human body and their functions and understand that living things reproduce.

Most young children are interested in their own bodies and their developing physical abilities. They should enjoy activities which enable them to understand and measure simple differences between themselves and other boys and girls in the class.

Level 1

Differences between children

What you need
Posters, six jars, foodstuffs, a blindfold, six assorted shapes, six assorted objects with different aromas.

What to do
Stress the point that children differ in their physical abilities by comparing the senses of the children in the class.

● Which of the children can see the best? Put a simple poster on the wall. How close does each child have to come in order to read all the words on it?

● Who has the keenest hearing? Whisper a sentence into the ear of each child. Who can hear it from the greatest distance?

● Who has the most acute sense of taste? Prepare six jars, each containing some food with a distinctive taste. Blindfold each child in turn. Using a clean spoon each time, give the blindfolded child a small portion of the food to identify, taking samples from each jar in turn. Keep swapping the order of the jars. How many children can recognize all six tastes?

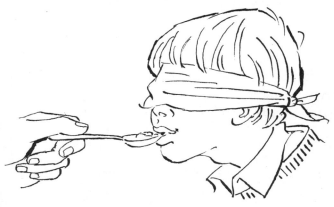

● Perform similar blindfold tests with six pungent aromas and six distinctive shapes. Use these activities as the introduction to a description of the various organs associated with our senses – eyes, ears, tongue, nose and skin.

Follow-up
Emphasis the fact that individuals vary one from the other by discussing variations between animals. Ask the children about their pets and encourage them to bring them to school where possible.

How do these pets differ from the children themselves? What are the differences in feeding habits, movement, and so on? See if the children, under supervision at home, can keep a record of the feeding habits and rates of growth of their pets. Ask them to bring the records to school for discussion.

Level 2

Measuring differences
What you need
Pencils, paper, a video showing people from different countries, items of clothing from around the world, dried peas.

What to do

Once the children are used to the idea of comparing things, ask them to make comparisons among themselves, measuring and recording the results. What are their likes and dislikes? How do their clothes differ? What differences in appearance are there among children in the class?

● Show the children pictures and videos of people around the world. Discuss the similarities and differences. What would the children wear for different activities and in different climates around the world?

● Ask the children to make a record of the basic measurements of everyone in the class, using both standard and non-standard units of measurement:

Height
Weight
Chest
Waist
Hand span
Foot length
Colour of eyes
Colour of hair.

This information could be used for a series of wall-charts:

Tallest child
Shortest child
Number of children with blue eyes
Number of children with brown hair.

● The process of comparison can be developed in a number of ways. How many peas can each child pick up with one hand? How well can the children walk along a straight line chalked on the floor? Who is the fastest runner in the class? Who can jump the farthest?

● Once they have mastered the process of comparison, ask the children to work out a series of simple correlations. Is the biggest child the fastest runner? Does the child with the biggest hand pick up the most dried peas? Do children with brown eyes see better than children with blue eyes?

Information technology

● Use television programmes and videos to show the children how people differ from country to country.

● Ask the children to make a study of different forms of communication around the world. Stresss the fact that people speak many different languages.

● How do the children think messages are passed on in areas where there are few radios, television sets and other technological aids? How many ways can the children devise of passing on messages?

Cross-curricular activities

● Read aloud *The Six Bullerby Children* by Astrid Lindgren (Methuen). This is the story of

three boys and three girls who play together but are very different in many ways.
● Make a face montage and compare human features. Help the children to cut out pictures of different facial features − noses, ears and eyes − from magazines. Glue them on to sheets of paper to make faces.

Summary

Although we may look alike there are many differences between people. It is possible to test many of these differences.

**AT2: Life and living processes − D
(Human influences on the Earth)**

Involve the children in a number of activities in which they have to care for the environment. These activities will help them to understand how human activities can affect the Earth, sometimes for good and sometimes for bad.

Level 1

Man-made waste

What you need
Large cloth or tarpaulin, gloves, rubbish from the playground, dustbin or bin liners.

What to do
Involve the children in a project to keep the playground clean. Put a large cloth or tarpaulin on the floor of the classroom and ask the children to place on it all the rubbish they collect from the playground over a period of several days. Using gloves, the children should sort the rubbish into categories − tins, bottles, paper and so on. Supervise the children closely during this activity, and remove any potentially dangerous rubbish.
● Ask the cleaner if the children can watch the rubbish being disposed of into dustbins or bin liners. Complete the children's introduction to the disposal of waste by allowing them to watch from a safe distance when the rubbish disposal lorry arrives to collect the waste.
● Select a number of commonplace objects and ask the children to decide under what

circumstances these could be classed as waste. What is waste paper? Is there such a thing as waste wood? What other waste products are there? Could any of these be described as dangerous? How could they be made safe?

Follow-up
Ask the children to look around their homes and see what different waste products are thrown out in the course of a week. Can they think of any uses for these waste products?
    Let the children find out about ways of disposing of waste or recycling it.

Level 2

Natural waste
What you need
Tin, soil, worms, scraps of cheese, paper and metal, pencils, paper, cloth, videos showing fertilizer being spread over the land.

What to do
In order to show that living things produce waste and that this waste can be useful, fill a tin with earth and place some worms in it. Punch some holes in the lid, put the lid back on the tin and leave it for a week. During that time, the worms will have eaten some of the soil and passed it back out again through their bodies. The waste from their bodies will produce soil which is looser and easier for plants to grow in.

When the week is over, open the tin. Examine the changes in the soil. Discuss, assess and record them.
● Show the children − in reality or on video − fertilizers being used on the land. Discuss the reason for this.
● Demonstrate that some waste items decay naturally, but that sometimes this may take a long time. Place a number of different waste items including cheese, paper and metal on a cloth. Keep examining them. Do any of them decay? What can be done to help break down those waste items which remain the same?
● Encourage the children to make illustrated, written notes of the changes in the waste items after a month, two months and a term. Does it make any difference to the rate of decay in any of the waste items if they are left outside in the sun and rain?
● Launch a campaign to keep the school tidy. Compare natural waste with that left by people. Do different times of the year produce their own particular types of waste, both natural and man-made?

Information technology
Use a thermometer to record the temperature at different times of the year to see if heat hastens decay in foodstuffs. How might this rate of decay be slowed down?

Cross-curricular activities
● Read *Stig of the Dump* by Clive King (Puffin). This is the story of a boy and the stone-age man he finds living in a rubbish dump, who recycles things in order to keep alive.
● Ask the children to make a junk model animal, using old tins, paper cups, string, card and glue.
● Make a graph showing the most common types of waste and rubbish found in the classroom.

Summary
● Living things die and decay.
● All living things give off certain waste products.
● Some sorts of waste may be harmful if not treated or disposed of.

CHEESE   BREAD   METAL   PAPER   APPLE   MILK   PLASTIC

Use the following activities to give the children an opportunity to study weather and some of its varying effects on the Earth and on our lives.

Level 1

Weather

What you need
Pictures of different weather conditions.

What to do
As an introduction to the study of weather, let the children collect pictures of different kinds of weather conditions. In class, talk about the pictures. Compare the pictures with the weather outside the classroom, and ask the children to describe the sort of weather they like best.

This activity could be used as an introduction to studying changes in the weather, weather conditions around the world, and the effects that various weather conditions can have on homes and buildings. Can the children think of any other effects of weather?

Level 2

Seasonal changes

What you need
Clothing appropriate to the different seasons, water, container.

What to do
Ask the children to collect some clothes for each of the four seasons, giving reasons for their choices. What sort of weather do they expect in each season?

Follow-up
Freeze some water in a container, and use it to demonstrate why ice is not a safe surface on which to drive or walk – this could form part of a project on road safety. Use ice again to show one of the effects of the sun in summer. Spring can act as a springboard for all sorts of appropriate seasonal work; try growing some plants in the classroom as part of an activity on new life.

People and weather
What you need
Two milk bottles, warm water, ice-cubes, toy ship, toy farm animals, hair-dryer.

What to do

Heat two milk bottles by filling them with warm water. Let the children pour away most of the water, and place an ice-cube on top of one bottle. What happens to the bottle with the ice-cube on top? What happens to the other bottle? How have they managed to make mist? Can the children think of ways in which mist affects people's lives?

● Let the children place some ice-cubes in a bowl of water and float a toy ship among them. Discuss with the children the ways in which ice might affect people's lives. What dangers might it hold for people on board a ship?

● Let the children make a toy farm, and then use a hair-drier to simulate the effects of wind on the animals, people and buildings. Ask the children how strong winds might affect people's lives. Is the wind ever beneficial?

Recording the weather

What you need

Coloured paper, gummed paper, scissors, pencils, plastic container.

What to do

Make a weather chart for the classroom, using squares of a different colour for each day of the school week. Cut out a number of weather symbols on sticky paper — an umbrella for rain, a cloud for a dull day and so on. Ask the children to devise and draw some symbols for sun, fog, snow, wind and any other weather condition they can think of.

Take the children outside each day and ask them which symbol should be stuck on that day's square. At the end of each month, construct a wall chart showing the weather conditions for the previous four weeks, under the headings 'Number of rainy days', 'Number of sunny days', and so on. At the end of the term, work out which months were predominantly wet, and which dry.

Help the children to construct a weather vane, and keep recordings of the direction of the wind. Use a plastic container firmly embedded in the ground to measure the rainfall for a short period — perhaps a week or a month.

Monday	
Tuesday	
Wednesday	
Thursday	
Friday	

Information technology

● What forms of information technology are used in the gathering and passing on of information about the weather?

● Give the children a brief outline of the function of weather ships and satellites.

● Show them a televised weather forecast and ask them to prepare and deliver their own forecasts, using their own weather vanes and rainfall gauges.

Cross-curricular activities

● Read the children a number of stories involving the weather, including *Topsy and Tim's Foggy Day* by Jean and Gareth Adamson (Blackie), *The Little Fir Tree* by Hans Andersen from any edition of his fairy tales, and *Moominland Midwinter* by Tove Jansson (Puffin).

● Place a large outline map of Great Britain on the classroom wall. Each day, read to the children the daily newspapers weather forecast for each retion. Let the children stick the appropriate weather symbols on the different parts of the map.

Summary

● Weather has a great effect upon the way in which we live. It changes from season to season.

● The sun gives us light and heat.

● Wind is moving air.

● Rain and snow are both forms of falling water.

The concept of the Earth as part of the solar system will be dealt with in more detail on page 116, but at this stage the children should be made aware that the Sun, Moon and Earth are separate bodies, and they should also be introduced to the study of the seasons and day and night.

Level 1

Seasonal changes
What you need
Small ball, pencils, paper, pegs.

What to do
Encourage the children to 'adopt' an area of open land near the school which contains grass, trees and bushes. See that they visit this area in each of the seasons and keep a diary recording the changes from season to season.
● Ask the children to go out into the playground on a number of occasions over the course of a few days. Is there a time on most days when the playground seems warmer than at other times? Does this have anything to do with the position of the Sun overhead?
● Explain how day and night occur by moving a small ball, to stand for the Earth, around a fixed light from a lamp, representing the Sun. In the same manner, explain how the seasons occur.

Motion of the sun
What you need
Sticks, pegs, clock.

What to do
On a sunny day, push a stick into the ground so that it casts a shadow. Every hour, take the children outside and mark with a peg where the tip of the shadow falls. Each peg should mark a different hour. For a few days, compare the time according to the shadow clock with that from a mechanical clock. Explain that the movement of the Earth around the Sun has enabled us to make a clock which tells the time. How can we use this clock?

Level 2

Night and day

What you need
Spinning top, pencils, paper.

What to do
Explain how night occurs by spinning a top around a stationary light.

Explain to the children that the length of a day changes during the year. Over a period of twelve months, measure the amount of daylight each day. Establish that the nights grow longer in the winter.

Date	Sunrise & Sunset times	
1st Jan.		
1st Feb.		
1st Mar.		
1st Apr.		
1st May		
1st June		
1st July		
1st Aug.		
1st Sept.		

Sun, Moon and Earth

What you need
Lightbulb, bulbholder, globe, tissue paper.

What to do
In order to study the Sun and Earth and to establish that they are separate bodies, show the children an electric lightbulb in a holder. Ask them to imagine that the bulb is the Sun. In front of the bulb, place a small globe to represent the Earth, on which we live. Hold a sheet of tissue paper between the light and the globe. Does it make any difference to the strength of the light shining on the globe?

Repeat the experiment with ten, twenty and more sheets of tissue paper. How many pieces of paper have to be held up before the light fails to shine on the globe? This is similar to what happens on a dull day. The atmosphere is not clear, but the sun is shining just as brightly as it does on a sunny day.

Information technology
Use television programmes and videos on communications to show how information passes quickly around the Earth.

Cross-curricular activities
● Introduce the children to books about the Earth, the Sun, the Moon and the seasons, such as *I Want to See the Moon* by Louis Baum (Bodley Head), *The Boy Who Painted the Sun*, by Jill Morris (Viking Kestrel), and *Stories for Summer*, by Alf Proysen (Hutchinson).
● Ask the children to prepare a folder on the different seasons. They could make a collection of pressed flowers, leaves and grasses for each of the seasons of the year, and write about them. Press the collected objects between sheets of blotting paper, then stick them on to cards marked spring, summer, autumn and winter.

Summary
● The Earth travels round the Sun.
● This movement gives us both day and night and the seasons.
● The four seasons are spring, summer, autumn and winter.

The children should be encouraged to be inquisitive about their surroundings, noting the shape, colour and texture of everything around them.

Level 1

Take the children round the houses and other buildings in the neighbourhood. What shapes are they? Are there any buildings shaped like a square, a triangle, a rectangle, a circle? Compare the shapes of doors and windows in the same way. What materials are the buildings made of? Show the children objects made of wood, stone, glass, plastic and brick, and encourage them to touch these objects. Use the following activity to help them describe objects by their simple properties.

Describing objects
What you need
Different types of wallpaper.

What to do
Ask the children to bring some scraps of wallpaper to school; try to collect as many different types as possible. Let them examine and handle all the pieces and compare their sizes, shapes, colours, patterns and textures.

Which kind would they like to use on the walls of their class? Can they design and make their own wallpaper?

Level 2

Various tests could be applied to a selection of different sorts of wallpaper. What happens when the pieces of wallpaper are torn, stretched, crumpled and folded?

Repeat these comparisons with other materials; use different kinds of cloth, perhaps including light cotton, scraps of carpet, curtain material and so on.

Grouping materials
What you need
Different types of metal, soft cloths.

What to do
This activity will encourage children to group materials according to their characteristics. Collect as many diffrent types of metal as possible (do not use pieces with jagged edges). Ask the children to polish the pieces with the cloths. Can they make all the metals shine, or only some of them? Do some achieve a shine more easily than others? Can they think of any special uses for shiny metals?

Conduct similar experiments with types of wood – smooth and coarse – or stones – rough and smooth, etc. Ask the children to suggest uses for these materials.

Heating and cooling
What you need
Ice-cubes, kettle, modelling clay, an assortment of objects which bounce, roll and bend, pencils, paper.

What to do
Demonstrate that heating and cooling may cause changes in materials by placing some water in the freezer compartment of a refrigerator. What has happened to the water? Place the ice-cubes in the sun, and observe what occurs. What happens when water boils? Ask the children to discuss these changes and write about them.

Which sorts of objects become hot when placed in the sun and which do not? Can the children think of any uses for a frozen ice-cube? Let the children work with modelling clay, and encourage them to describe the changes they make in the material as they handle it.

Follow-up
At this stage, the children should be given many opportunities to recognize similarities and differences in materials. Let them make collections of materials under various headings: 'Hard things', 'Soft things', 'Things which bounce', 'Things which bend', 'Things which roll'.

From this, the children could go on to find particular uses for rolling objects, bouncing objects, bending objects and so on.

Information technology
● As part of their experience in grouping and sorting, ask the children to make a list of objects which receive text, sound and images over long distances – television and radio, telephones and so on.
● Show the children how these instruments work, and emphasise the importance of observing the rules of safety when touching them.

Cross-curricular activities
● Read *The Borrowers* by Mary Norton (Dent/Puffin). This is the story of little creatures who live under the floorboards, sorting and using the debris left by people.
● Make a shell box, first collecting and sorting as many different kinds of shell as possible. Glue shells in patterns to the top of a cardboard box.
● Make a three-dimensional display of stones or metals.

Summary
● There are many different kinds of materials. They may be compared and sorted by shape, colour, texture, and in other ways.
● Materials react in different ways in various conditions, including heat and cold.

Help the children to appreciate that different types of force are needed for various situations, and that pushing, pulling and twisting are all important forces in movement.

Level 1

Take the children round the school. Ask them to demonstrate how often they have to push, pull, twist or lift things in order to make things happen in the course of a school day. How much force is needed for each object? Are any particular skills needed? Are there easier ways of achieving the required aim? Are some objects in the school too difficult for an infant to move? Should they be redesigned?

Pushing
What you need
Large cardboard boxes, toys on four wheels.

What to do
In order to show that things can be moved by pushing them, take some large cardboard boxes and, during PE or a games lesson, ask one or two children to sit inside each box. Under strict supervision, ask the other children to try to move the boxes. Which is the easiest way to move the boxes? Does the size or weight of the child inside make any difference to the amount of force needed?
● Give each child a toy with four wheels. Ask the children to move the toys over a variety of surfaces — rough, smooth, sloping, flat, and so on. Does the nature of the surface make any difference to the amount of force needed to push the toys?

Level 2

Pushing and pulling
What you need
Toy cars, ramp, toy sailing ship or matchboxes, Plasticine, spent matches, paper, hair-dryer, toy cart, assortment of elastic-powered, clockwork and electrical toys, bucket of water, floating and sinking objects.

What to do
To show that pushes and pulls can make things start moving, speed up, swerve or stop, let the children push model cars of different sizes down a ramp. How far do the cars go before they stop? Does the force of the push affect this? Does the size of the car affect it? Does altering the steepness of the ramp have any effect? How can the car be made to swerve as it leaves the ramp?

● Test the power of the wind to push a model sailing craft. Ask the children to make a small vessel out of a matchbox tray, with a small mast made from a used match fixed in position with Plasticine, and a paper sail. Turn on a hair-dryer and use this force to propel the vessel. Encourage the children to adjust the force of the dryer and operate it from different distances. Does the force of the wind affect the speed or direction of the craft? What happens when there is no wind?

● How many different ways can the children find of propelling a small model cart? Which is the easiest way? Does it make any difference if it is moved over different surfaces or slopes?

● Ask the children to bring as many toys as possible which are propelled by different types of power — by elastic, by clockwork and by electricity. What happens when the different forms of power are turned on or operated? What happens when they are turned off or stopped? Is it possible to increase or decrease the speed of any of these toys? How is this done?

Which forms of power enable the toys to swerve? How is this managed? Which forms of power are most effective in stopping a toy when required?

Study toys which spin, leap, rebound and fly. Work out the most effective form of propulsion in different circumstances; for example, when is it better to push than to pull?

● Set up an investigation into floating and sinking by collecting 20 small objects and filling a bucket with water. Ask the children to put the objects in the water one by one, and classify each object under one of the headings, 'Things that float' and 'Things that sink'.

Are there any similarities between the sinking objects? What seem to be the similarities between the floating objects? Can a sinking object be turned into a floating one by altering its shape? Encourage the children to experiment with this in as many ways as they can.

Information technology

● Discuss with the children the different kinds of forces which are needed to in order to operate computers, televisions, radios and other machines. Can the operation of these machines be slowed down or altered by the application of force? How can the machines be stopped?

● How many different forms of power can the children think of which can operate clocks and watches?

Cross-curricular activities

● Read aloud a number of fairy tales involving different forms of movement: *Jack and the Beanstalk* (climbing), *Cinderella* (dancing), *Puss in Boots* (walking).

● Let the children make a toy snail. First, find an empty snail shell. Make the body of the snail out of Plasticine. Stick the base of the Plasticine to a small piece of wood or thick cardboard. The children can then experiment with ways of moving the snail — for example by pushing and pulling.

Summary

● Force is needed to start something moving. The main ways of moving things are by carrying, sliding (pushing and pulling) and rolling.

● The stronger the force the sooner an object will move fast.

● The same amount of force will move a small object faster than a big one.

Great care should be taken to stress the importance of safety when you are introducing children to activities involving electricity and magnetism. Make sure that the children are familar with the following safety rules:

● Never conduct any experiment using mains electricity. Always use battery-powered apparatus.

● Never touch plugs or sockets with wet hands.

● Always remove the plug before filling an electric kettle.

● Never use worn or damaged flexes.

● Never pull an appliance by the flex.

● Never use a damaged plug.

● Never play with switches or sockets.

● Never use any electrical apparatus unless an adult is supervising.

● Use adaptors sparingly. Try to use a separate socket outlet for every appliance.

● Never play with kites or model aircraft near an overhead electricity wire or pylon.

Level 1

Electricity

What you need

Rubber comb, scraps of paper, woollen cloth, square of glass, tissue paper, silk cloth, pencils, paper.

What to do

Take the children around the school and show them everything you can find which is powered by electricity – lights, bells, telephones, television sets and machinery. Let them see how these objects are operated and turned off. Ask the children to find out what it is necessary to do in order to observe rules of safety when operating electrical objects.

● Bring into school a hard rubber comb, some small pieces of paper and some woollen cloth. Put the small pieces of paper on the table. Ask the children to rub the comb with the woollen cloth, which will cause it to pick up electrons from the cloth and become charged. Tell the

children that they are making electricity. Ask them to hold the comb close to the pieces of paper and then discuss and record what happens.

● Collect together a square of glass, some tissue paper and some silk cloth. Place the glass across two raised objects so that it is above the surface of the table. Tear the tissue paper into small pieces and put them on the table beneath the glass. Pick up the glass, rub it with the silk and replace it. Observe what happens. Ask the children to discuss and record this in the light of the results of the last experiment.

● Investigate the use of electricity to power household objects by looking at electric light and electric fires. What happens in each case when the electricity is turned off?

● Remind the children that they must pull out the plug before filling a kettle, and that they must not touch plugs or sockets with wet hands.

Level 2

Magnetism

What you need

Magnets, iron filings, matchsticks, elastic bands, metal objects which float, bucket, water, pin, paper.

What to do

Obtain a magnet, some iron filings and some other small objects, such as matchsticks and elastic bands. Ask the children to discover which objects are attracted by the magnet and which are not. Ask them to try to find as many objects as possible which they think will be attracted by a magnet.

● Make a classroom collection of different kinds of magnets. Let the children experiment with them all. Which are the most effective and which the least effective? Does the shape or size of a magnet seem to have any bearing on its effectiveness?

● Show the children how to use a magnet to attract pieces of metal floating in a container of water. Let them have a race, using several floating metal objects and two magnets operated from above.

● Place a pin on a sheet of paper. Hold a magnet beneath the paper and make the pin travel across the surface of the paper. Can the children invent a game of their own, based on this principle?

● Ask the children to use a magnet to find some magnetic objects which have been mixed up with non-magnetic ones. Let them try to make a pin leap through the air by slowly sliding a magnet towards it. Which child can make the most objects dangle from a magnet?

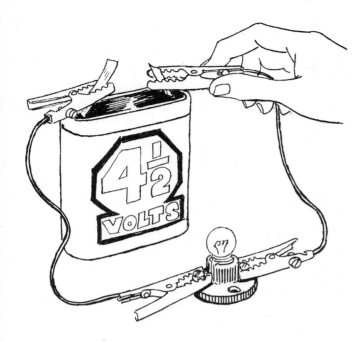

Conducting electricity
What you need
Copper wires, battery, electric bulb, pieces of rubber, silk cloth, wood, crocodile clips.

What to do
Show a small group of children at a time how to construct an electrical circuit. Take care to emphasise the safety aspects. Take away the insulation from the end of the copper wires. Attach the battery to the bulb, but use two short pieces of wire on one side, so that there is a gap in the circuit. Let the children bring the two ends of the wire together to complete the circuit and light the bulb. Then they can try holding the rubber, the silk and the wood between the two ends of the wire. What effect does each object have on the lighting of the bulb? Which objects conduct electricity and which do not?

How can this knowledge be used to ensure the safe use of electricity?

Information technology
● Show the children how to use a morse code transmitter powered by electricity.
● Are there other ways of passing on messages which do not involve speaking?

Cross-curricular activities
● To demonstrate some inventive uses of electricity and many other forms of power, read the children *The Incredible Adventures of Professor Branestawm* by Norman Hunter (Bodley Head).
● Make a number of different insects by twisting and joining together lengths of thin, soft iron wire. Use a magnet to draw the insects across a surface.
● Give the children practice in using the telephone, making up messages in advance or speaking spontaneously on a given theme.

Summary
● Electricity cannot be seen but it is all around us. It is used to power objects and may be turned on or off with a switch. It may be stored in a battery.
● It can be dangerous and must be handled with care. Never experiment with mains electricity.

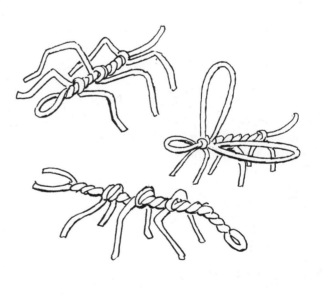

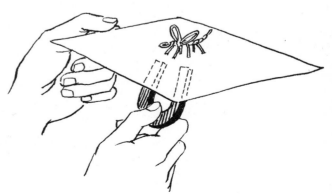

Energy is not an easy topic for young children to understand, but with plenty of practical activities they should be able to grasp that energy is important in the movement of people and objects, that food plays a vital part in providing energy for living things and that in living things and in inanimate objects energy may be stored and transferred.

Level 1

Gathering energy
What you need
Pencils, paper.

What to do
Show the children that the more energy they have the faster and stronger they can become. Organise a series of races across the playground to discover the fastest runners in the class. See who can jump the furthest from a standing start. The children can then make notes of their findings, and display the results on wall charts under headings such as 'Fastest runners' and 'Best jumpers'.
● After a PE session, let the children measure the increase in their heartbeat and breathing rates.

● Help the children discover that people need food in order to be active. Talk about different types of food, and find out the most popular foods in the class. The children can then work out a series of menus for breakfast, lunch and tea. Let the children help feed the classroom pets and observe their eating habits.
● Work out roughly how much sleep each child in the class has each night. Ask the children at which times of day they feel most energetic. Can they see a reason for this?

Level 2

Hot and cold
What you need
Pencils, paper.

What to do
In order to understand the meaning of hot and cold in relation to the temperature of their bodies, the children could make two lists; one of warm places in the school and one of cold places. Which places do the children find most comfortable? How does it feel when they stand for a while in a cold place? How does it feel to stand in a hot place?

Do the children find it easier to work in warm places or in cold ones? Can they think of any ways of making cold places warmer and warm places cooler? Talk about ways of keeping warm when it is cold. How do warm clothes help? Can the children think of any reasons why exercises warm us up? Do they know any good ways to cool down?

Storing and releasing energy

What you need
Elastic bands, pencils, rulers, matchboxes, coins.

What to do
Ask each child to twist an elastic band around a pencil until it is tight. Energy has been stored in the elastic band, and it can be released by letting go of the band. Can the children construct a simple toy using this principle?

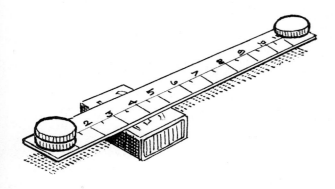

At this level, the children should be introduced to the use of levers, which enable people to use a little energy to do a lot of work. Balance a ruler across a matchbox so that the short end sticks out over one side and the long end over the other. Place two coins on top of one another on the tip of the short end of the ruler. Then balance one coin of a similar sort on the tip of the long end. What does the one coin do to the two coins? Why has this happened? Could the children make a toy see-saw using this principle?

Information technology
● Ask the children to study the ways in which different forms of energy may be used to pass on a message. A note tied to a stone could be thrown (very carefully) from child to child. A note tied to a piece of wood could be propelled from a catapult.
● Electricity is used to power radio and television sets.

Cross-curricular activities
● Introduce the children to the following books which feature eating: *The Very Hungry Caterpillar* by Eric Carle (Heinemann/Puffin), *War and Peas* by Michael Foreman (Puffin), and *The Supermarket Mice* by Margaret Gordon (Puffin).
● Make a spinning buzzer. Glue two paper plates together. Make two holes near the centre of the plates. Pass a loop of string through the two holes and tie the ends of the string together. Twist the string, thus storing energy, and spin the plates by exerting and relaxing the pressure on the string. If the edges of the plates are notched, the spinning disc will make a buzzing sound.

Summary
● Energy is the power which makes things move.
● Food provides the energy used by people.
● Energy can be stored and then used.

Sound and music can be linked with a number of other subjects in the curriculum. As the children experiment with and make sounds, let them learn to play simple musical instruments, and discover what happens when sound passes through different materials.

Level 1

Variety of sounds

What you need
Pencils, paper, guitar, matchboxes, elastic bands, long-stemmed wine glass.

What to do
Ask the children to keep a diary of all the sounds they hear during one day. Ask them to assess these sounds and list them under different headings: 'Loud sounds', 'Soft sounds', 'Pleasant sounds', 'Unpleasant sounds', 'Sounds made by people', 'Sounds made by animals' and 'Sounds made by machines'.

● Help the children to appreciate that sounds can be made in a variety of ways. Sounds are caused by vibrations or movements through the air. Pluck one of the strings of a guitar. Ask the children to watch the string and listen to what happens after the string has been plucked.
● Give each child a matchbox with an elastic band wound round it. Let each child pluck the band and listen for the vibration. What can they see, hear and feel?
● Wet a finger and rub it round the rim of a long-stemmed wine glass. What can the children hear?
● Ask each child in turn to say something, and to put a hand on his or her throat at the same time. The children should feel their vocal chords moving. Ask them what these chords seem to be doing. Can they see how this compares with the previous activities?
● Let the children make sounds in many different ways and discuss how they produce the sounds. Ask them to list the uses of different sounds — as warnings, to give information, for pleasure, and so on.

Level 2

Hearing sounds

What you need
Basin, water, stone, guitar.

What to do
Sounds are heard when vibrations reach the ear. Illustrate this by filling a basin with water and dropping a stone in the water. Ask the children to watch the circles spreading outwards in the water. This is something like the way in which we hear things. The vibration of an object causes sound waves which spread until they reach the ear.

Using a guitar, find out which notes the children can hear most easily at different distances.

Musical sounds

What you need
Assorted containers, dried peas, marbles, wooden spoons, combs, grease-proof paper, musical instruments.

What to do
Display a variety of simple musical instruments, and allow the children to practise making sounds on them. Let the children make and use their own simple musical instruments. They can make shakers by filling tins, boxes and other containers with dried peas or marbles, and construct drums from a variety of containers, using wooden spoons for beaters. Let the children beat the spoons on a range of different surfaces around the classroom. They can also make a mouth organ by blowing through a comb wrapped round with grease-proof paper.
● Let the children find out which objects muffle sound and which allow it to travel. Are some musical instruments more piercing than others? If so, why is this? Can the chldren hear a radio playing through the following barriers: a thick wall; a thin wall; a blanket; an open window; a closed window?
● How can noise annoy people? What precautions should be taken to avoid noise troubling neighbours?

Information technology
Examine the forms of information technology which rely mainly on sounds to pass on their messages. Study radios, tape-recorders, cassette players and so on, observing their similarities and differences.

Cross-curricular activities
● Introduce the children to books featuring sounds and music, including perhaps *Patrick* by Quentin Blake (Cape/Puffin), *Moo, Baa, La La La* by Sandra Boynton (Methuen) and *Little Bear and the Oompah-Pah* by Francesca Crespi (Methuen).
● Let the children make and decorate their own shakers. First they should put some clean milk-bottle tops in an old cocoa tin, and then they can decorate the outside of the tin. Ask them to compare the sounds made by different shakers.

Summary
● Sounds are caused by vibrations or shaking. Different vibrations cause different sounds.
● We hear sounds with the part of our ear called the ear-drum. The ear-drum vibrates when it picks up a sound.

The examination of the origins of light, the colour all around us, reflections and shadows provides plenty of opportunities for practical work and attractive display.

Level 1

Take the children round the school, showing them examples of objects which give off their own light: the sun, candles, fire, torches and matches. Make a collection of different types of torches, but show that each operates in the same basic way.

Ask the children to count the number of different colours they can find in the school. Explain that light comprises three basic, or *primary*, colours: red, green and violet. (The children will be interested to know that this differs from the primary colours for paint, which are red, yellow and blue.) Go round the school again and ask the children to list the things they see under the headings, 'Red objects', 'Green objects' and 'Violet objects'.

Sources of light
What you need
Candles, lanterns, globe, torch.

What to do
Demonstrate that light comes from different sources by making a collection of objects which give off light, such as candles and lanterns. Demonstrate how each one works. What would our lives be like without any light? Could we cope at school in the dark?
● Examine the strength of the sun at different times of the day and at different times of the year. *Never* look directly at the sun with the naked eye. Simulate the action of the sun by shining a torch on to a moving globe.

Mixing colours
What you need
Thick card, coloured pencils, string, red, green and blue acetate film, white cardboard, three torches, painters' charts.

What to do

In order to match colours and discriminate between them, let the children make a spinning spectrum. First they should cut a piece of thick cardboard into a circle about eight centimetres in diameter and divide the circle into seven equal sections. Then they can colour each section a different colour of the spectrum: red, orange, yellow, green, blue, indigo and violet. Bore two small holes in the centre of the circle, and thread a piece of string about eight centimetres long through the two holes. Tie the ends of the string in a loop. Ask the children to name the seven colours. What seems to happen to these colours when the string is wound up and then released to spin the circle?

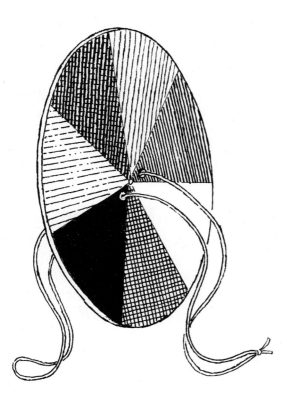

● Tie a piece of red acetate film over the head of one torch, green over another and blue over the third. Shine the torches on to a piece of white cardboard. Which colour emerges when all three torches are shone on the same spot at once? What colours can be made by using combinations of the torches, two at a time?

Discuss primary colours with the children.
● Use painters' charts to give the children practice in picking out different colours. Ask them to mix different colours and discuss the results. Can they invent and name a colour?

Camouflage
What you need
Small red and green pegs, pictures of animal camouflage.

What to do
For a study of colour in the environment, take the children out into a field. Scatter some small red pegs on the grass. Ask the children to collect them. Then ask the children to find and gather a similar number of green pegs scattered on the grass. Which were the easiest to find? Why? How do birds, animals and insects use this principle in order to avoid being seen?

Collect pictures of animal camouflage. Show the children some camouflage jackets against appropriate backgrounds.

Level 2

Path of light
What you need
Torch, clear and frosted glass, block of wood.

What to do
To show that light passes through some materials and not through others, shine a powerful torch through a piece of clear glass. Can the children see the beam clearly, hazily or not at all? Repeat the experiment with a piece of frosted glass and then a block of wood, asking the same questions. Introduce the children to the words transparent (allows light through), translucent (allows some light through) and opaque (allows no light through).
● Let the children experiment with the formation of shadows. Ask them to examine a number of objects and materials, putting each one under the headings transparent, translucent or opaque. Which of these objects can cast shadows? What does this mean?

Reflections

What you need

Assortment of transparent and translucent objects, paper, pencils, mirrors.

What to do

Explain that we see our reflections in a mirror because the surface is highly polished. Ask the children to find out how well they can see their reflections in a number of transparent and translucent objects, including puddles, metals and glass.

● Experiment with reflections in a mirror and the reversal of images. Ask each child to write something down and hold it in front of a mirror. What does the writing look like in the mirror? What does this mean? Do we get a true reflection of ourselves in a full-length mirror?

Information technology

● Show the children how a flashing mirror can be used to pass on messages.
● Tell them about the smoke signals used by the American Indians.
● How could light be used to pass on messages today?

Cross-curricular activities

● Introduce the children to these books with light and dark as their theme: *The Moon's Revenge* by Joan Aiken and Alan Lee (Cape), *After Dark* by Louis Baum (Andersen Press) and *The Silver Christmas Tree* by Pat Hutchins (Puffin).
● Using a large screen and a torch, cast a range of shadows on to the screen. Ask the children to draw silhouettes using these shadows as a guide.

Summary

● Most of our light comes from the Sun.
● The three primary colours are red, green and blue.
● Light passes through some objects but not through others.
● Shadows are formed when light does not pass through an object.

Chapter Two

Science-based projects

The science curriculum can be covered through an examination of each of the individual attainment targets more or less in isolation. Properly planned and executed, this method may suit many teachers.

There is, however, the possibility that such an approach may sometimes seem too fragmented. In that case, it will always be possible to combine a number of attainment

targets in one project or topic web. If such a project is scheduled to occupy half a term, then it should be possible to cover all the targets in the course of six projects spread over the school year.

Any combination of attainment targets is possible but in this chapter they have been grouped in four different projects, as listed overleaf.

Projects on living things
AT1: Scientific investigation
AT2: Life and living processes

Projects on the Earth and its materials
AT1: Scientific investigations
AT3: Earth and environment
AT4: Materials and their behaviour

Projects on forms of power
AT1 Scientific investigation
AT5: Energy and its effects

Projects on things around us
AT1: Scientific investigation
AT3: Earth and environment
AT5: Energy and its effects

Projects on living things

The projects on living things which are suggested here are 'Myself', 'Families' and 'The senses'.
● 'Myself' considers the similarities and differences between children, the conditions children need in order to live, the parts of the body, breathing, and inheritance and evolution.
● 'Families' looks at the variety of living things, reproduction, the growth of a baby and its needs, differences between children and differences between animals.
● 'The senses' begins by looking at children's senses, and considers safety precautions involving the senses, a study of the sense organs, different ways of testing and measuring children's reactions to a number of stimuli, the variety of animal movements and animal alertness.

Projects on living things: Myself (AT2: Life and living processes)

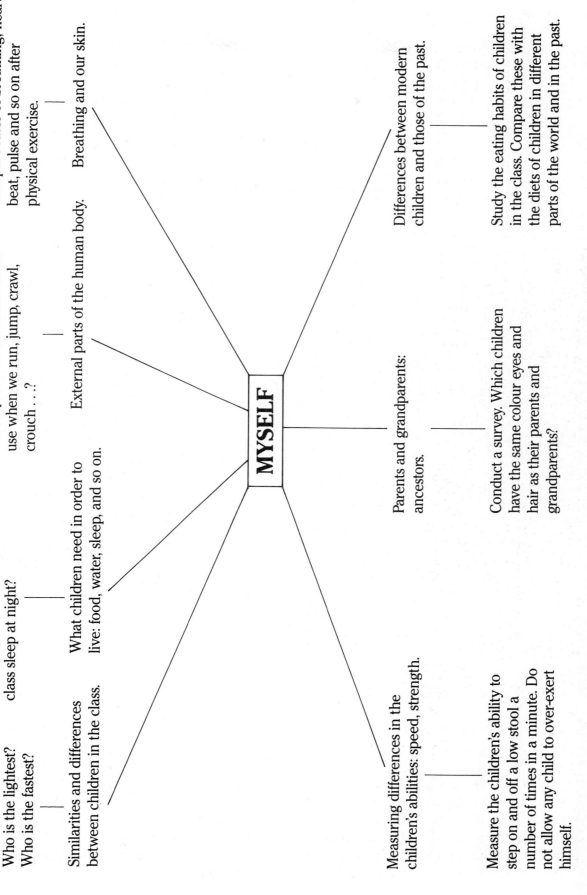

Who is the tallest?
Who is the lightest?
Who is the fastest?

How long does each child in the class sleep at night?

Compare rates of breathing, heart-beat, pulse and so on after physical exercise.

Breathing and our skin.

Which parts of our bodies do we use when we run, jump, crawl, crouch . . .?

External parts of the human body.

Differences between modern children and those of the past.

Study the eating habits of children in the class. Compare these with the diets of children in different parts of the world and in the past.

Similarities and differences between children in the class.

What children need in order to live: food, water, sleep, and so on.

MYSELF

Parents and grandparents: ancestors.

Conduct a survey. Which children have the same colour eyes and hair as their parents and grandparents?

Measuring differences in the children's abilities: speed, strength.

Measure the children's ability to step on and off a low stool a number of times in a minute. Do not allow any child to over-exert himself.

41

Projects on living things: Families (AT2: Life and living processes)

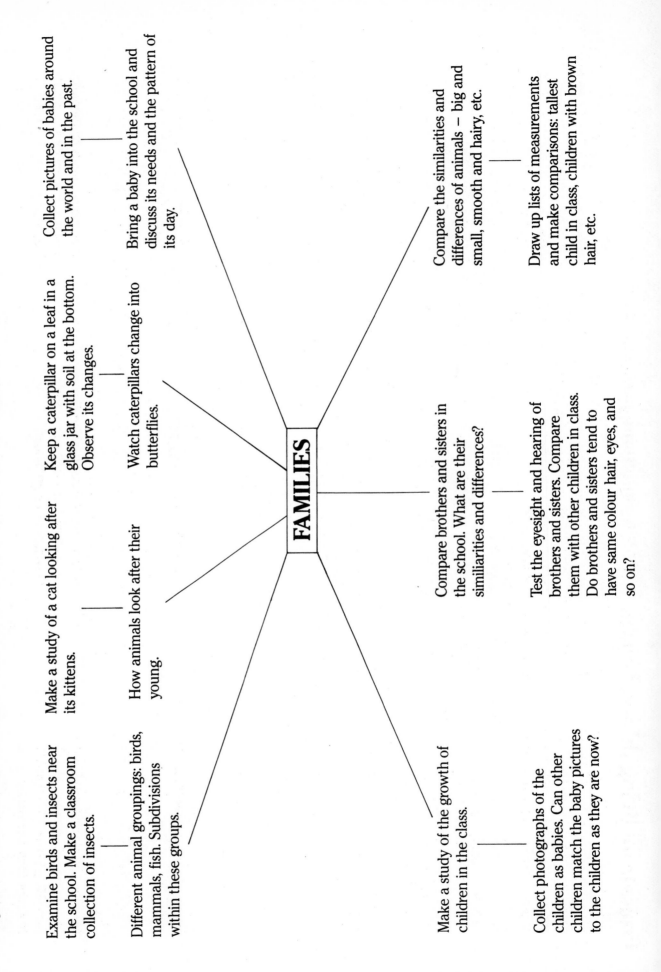

FAMILIES

Collect pictures of babies around the world and in the past.

Bring a baby into the school and discuss its needs and the pattern of its day.

Keep a caterpillar on a leaf in a glass jar with soil at the bottom. Observe its changes.

Watch caterpillars change into butterflies.

Make a study of a cat looking after its kittens.

How animals look after their young.

Examine birds and insects near the school. Make a classroom collection of insects.

Different animal groupings: birds, mammals, fish. Subdivisions within these groups.

Compare the similarities and differences of animals – big and small, smooth and hairy, etc.

Draw up lists of measurements and make comparisons: tallest child in class, children with brown hair, etc.

Compare brothers and sisters in the school. What are their similarities and differences?

Test the eyesight and hearing of brothers and sisters. Compare them with other children in class. Do brothers and sisters tend to have same colour hair, eyes, and so on?

Make a study of the growth of children in the class.

Collect photographs of the children as babies. Can other children match the baby pictures to the children as they are now?

Projects on living things: Senses (AT2: Life and living processes)

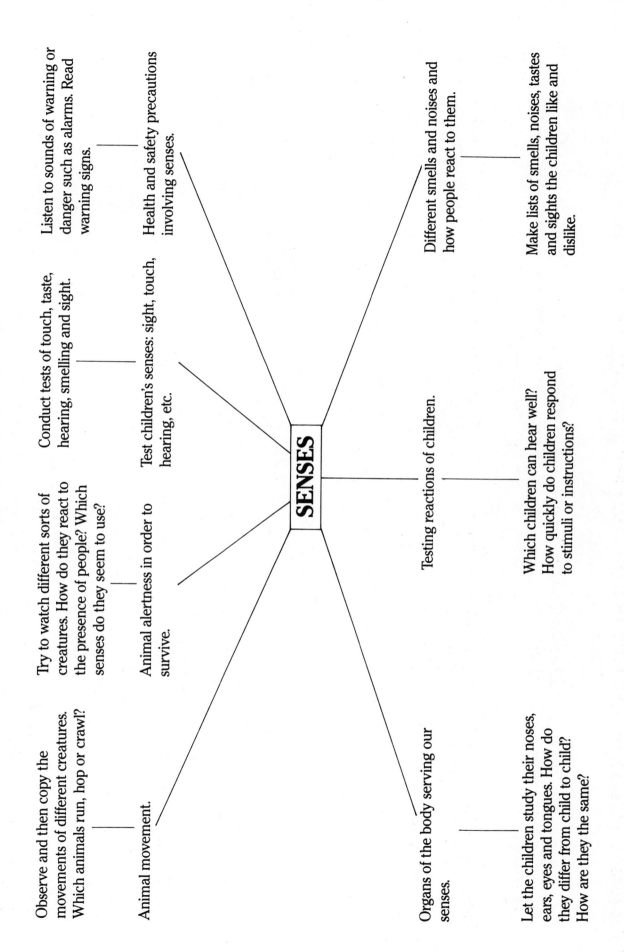

Listen to sounds of warning or danger such as alarms. Read warning signs.

Health and safety precautions involving senses.

Different smells and noises and how people react to them.

Make lists of smells, noises, tastes and sights the children like and dislike.

Conduct tests of touch, taste, hearing, smelling and sight.

Test children's senses: sight, touch, hearing, etc.

Try to watch different sorts of creatures. How do they react to the presence of people? Which senses do they seem to use?

Animal alertness in order to survive.

SENSES

Testing reactions of children.

Which children can hear well? How quickly do children respond to stimuli or instructions?

Observe and then copy the movements of different creatures. Which animals run, hop or crawl?

Animal movement.

Organs of the body serving our senses.

Let the children study their noses, ears, eyes and tongues. How do they differ from child to child? How are they the same?

Projects on the Earth and its materials

The projects suggested here for the subject of the Earth and its materials are 'School', 'Homes' and 'Holidays'.

● 'School' is a topic web which involves investigating different aspects of man-made waste and the ways in which it can be recycled, the structure of the school buildings, ways of measuring and comparing weather conditions and seasonal changes.

● 'Homes' covers work on rubbish in the street and at home, types of building materials and the effect that weathering has on them, the materials most suited to particular climates and weather conditions and, finally, types of homes made by animals.

● 'Holidays' looks at the pollution of beaches, seas and beauty spots, the building of sandcastles, the properties of sand and how it compares with other soils, weather charts and the importance of weather in our lives, the different types of holidays for different seasons, and the effects of the sun.

Projects on the Earth and its materials: School (AT3: Earth and environment) (AT4: Materials and their behaviour)

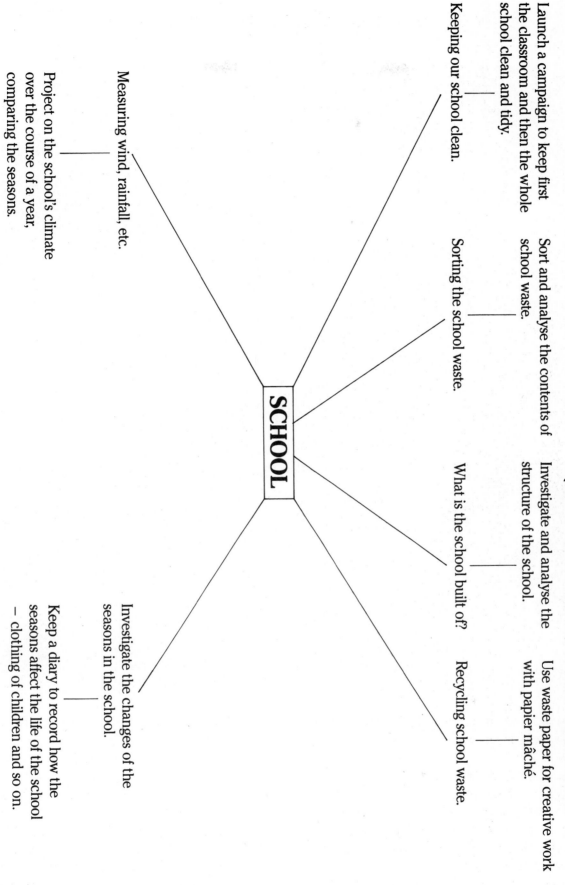

Launch a campaign to keep first the classroom and then the whole school clean and tidy.

Keeping our school clean.

Sorting the school waste.

Sort and analyse the contents of school waste.

What is the school built of?

Investigate and analyse the structure of the school.

Recycling school waste.

Use waste paper for creative work with papier mâché.

SCHOOL

Measuring wind, rainfall, etc.

Project on the school's climate over the course of a year, comparing the seasons.

Investigate the changes of the seasons in the school.

Keep a diary to record how the seasons affect the life of the school — clothing of children and so on.

Projects on the Earth and its materials: Homes (AT3: Earth and environment) (AT4: Materials and their behaviour)

HOMES

Sort the different types of rubbish. What are the most common sorts in most homes?

Different types of rubbish in the home.

Launch an anti-litter campaign in the home.

Disposing of rubbish in home and street.

Collect different types of brick, wood and other building materials.

Note the effects of weathering and erosion in and around the school.

Different types of building material.

Weathering and erosion.

Design a home for protection against sun, wind and rain.

Using building blocks, experiment with building a house that will withstand wind from an air current of some sort, such as a hair-drier.

Design a house with a roof which will not collect water when sprinkled with a water can.

What sort of homes do animals make? Can the children build their own bird's nest?

Animal homes.

Study buildings for different climates and weather conditions.

Use a thermometer to determine temperature, testing jars of water of differing warmth. What sort of house would be built in a hot area? What sort of house would be built in a cold one? Collect pictures of homes around the world.

Projects on the Earth and its materials: Holidays (AT3: Earth and environment) (AT4: Materials and their behaviour)

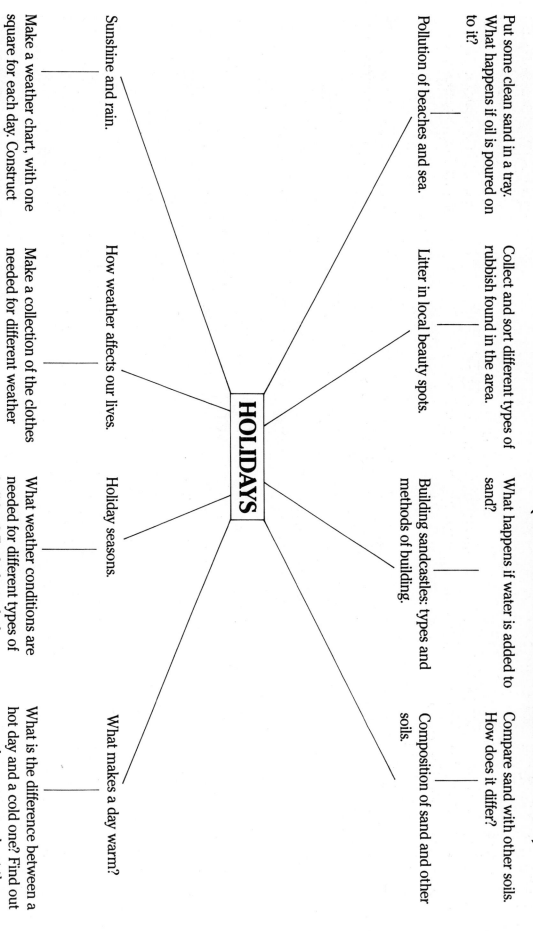

HOLIDAYS

Collect and sort different types of rubbish found in the area.

Put some clean sand in a tray. What happens if oil is poured on to it?

Pollution of beaches and sea.

Litter in local beauty spots.

What happens if water is added to sand?

Compare sand with other soils. How does it differ?

Building sandcastles: types and methods of building.

Composition of sand and other soils.

Sunshine and rain.

How weather affects our lives.

Holiday seasons.

What makes a day warm?

Make a weather chart, with one square for each day. Construct symbols to fill squares – umbrella symbols for rain, etc.

Make a collection of the clothes needed for different weather conditions.

What weather conditions are needed for different types of holidays? Each day, ask the children what sort of holiday they could go on, according to the weather.

What is the difference between a hot day and a cold one? Find out as much as you can about the sun.

47

Projects on forms of power

Projects which cover the topic of different sorts of power are 'Toys', 'Shapes' and 'Forces'.

● 'Toys' looks at making and comparing moving, floating and sinking toys, electricity and magnetism as means of moving toys, and the different mechanisms involved in making a toy move.

● 'Shapes' shows how shape determines function and movement. It also looks at the importance of shape in floating and sinking, in the construction of gears and in making an electrical circuit.

● 'Forces' examines children's movements and toys with simple mechanisms (to show how forces act upon objects), the different functions of electricity at home and at school, safety measures, sources of energy and how energy is transferred in toys.

Projects on forms of power: Toys (AT5: Energy and its effects)

Make a model spinning top by putting a pencil through a cardboard circle or square.

Make your own moving toy.

Put a piece of clay in water and watch it sink. Then fashion the wet clay into the shape of a boat. What happens when it is placed in water?

Collect toy ships. How do they float?

Organize races of metal boats across water, attracted by a magnet.

Attracting toys with magnets.

Conduct a series of races. Which toys go the fastest? Which keep going the longest?

Collect and compare toys propelled by electricity.

TOYS

Gears in toys.

Compare toys which are propelled by the interaction of gears. What is the function of a gear?

Collect and compare toys with different forms of movement.

Hold a series of races between toys powered by different forces. Which forms of energy are the best for speed? Which seem the best for endurance?

Experiment with giving a toy different amounts of energy.

Wind up clockwork toys to the full, then half-way, then only a little. Compare the results when the toys are operated. Repeat the experiment with toys propelled by elastic, wind, etc.

49

Projects on forms of power: Shapes (AT5: Energy and its effects)

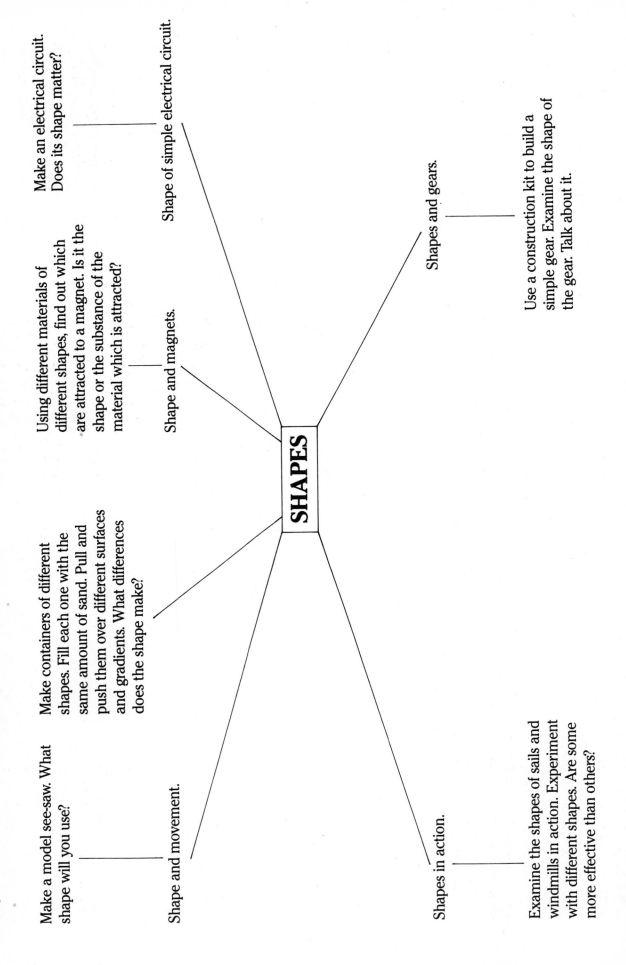

SHAPES

Make an electrical circuit. Does its shape matter?

Shape of simple electrical circuit.

Using different materials of different shapes, find out which are attracted to a magnet. Is it the shape or the substance of the material which is attracted?

Shape and magnets.

Shapes and gears.

Use a construction kit to build a simple gear. Examine the shape of the gear. Talk about it.

Make a model see-saw. What shape will you use?

Make containers of different shapes. Fill each one with the same amount of sand. Pull and push them over different surfaces and gradients. What differences does the shape make?

Shape and movement.

Shapes in action.

Examine the shapes of sails and windmills in action. Experiment with different shapes. Are some more effective than others?

Projects on forms of power: Forces (AT5: Energy and its effects)

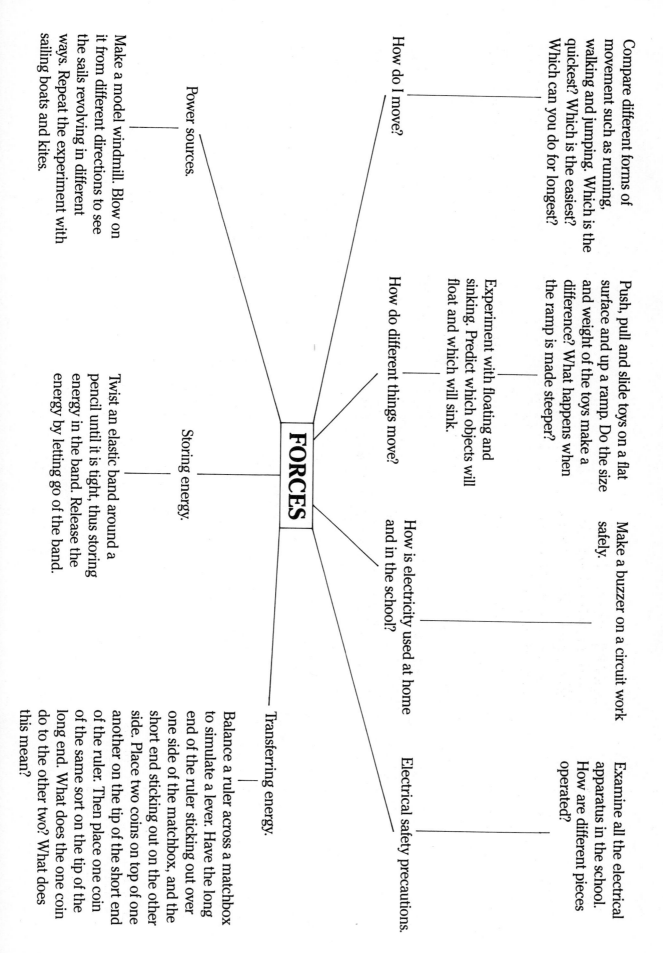

FORCES

How do I move?

Compare different forms of movement such as running, walking and jumping. Which is the quickest? Which is the easiest? Which can you do for longest?

Push, pull and slide toys on a flat surface and up a ramp. Do the size and weight of the toys make a difference? What happens when the ramp is made steeper?

How do different things move?

Experiment with floating and sinking. Predict which objects will float and which will sink.

Make a buzzer on a circuit work safely.

How is electricity used at home and in the school?

Examine all the electrical apparatus in the school. How are different pieces operated?

Electrical safety precautions.

Power sources.

Make a model windmill. Blow on it from different directions to see the sails revolving in different ways. Repeat the experiment with sailing boats and kites.

Storing energy.

Twist an elastic band around a pencil until it is tight, thus storing energy in the band. Release the energy by letting go of the band.

Transferring energy.

Balance a ruler across a matchbox to simulate a lever. Have the long end of the ruler sticking out over one side of the matchbox, and the short end sticking out on the other side. Place two coins on top of one another on the tip of the short end of the ruler. Then place one of the same sort on the tip of the long end. What does the one coin do to the other two? What does this mean?

51

Projects on things around us

The projects suggested here for the subject of things around us are 'Water', 'Travel' and 'Weather'.

● 'Water' covers work on the sounds of water, water and light, the significance of transparency and translucency, the origins of water and water in nature.

● 'Travel' looks at how sound and light travel, the different types of sound, noise pollution, how the Earth travels through the solar system and the journey of a rocket.

● 'Weather' includes work on the sounds that accompany weather conditions, signs that anticipate changes in the weather, the sun as a source of light and growth, and the importance of wind in weather patterns.

Projects on things around us: Water (AT3: Earth and environment) (AT5: Energy and its effects)

WATER

Water and light.

Does the look of the water have anything to do with its cleanliness?

Can water be changed from transparent to translucent to opaque? How?

Sounds made by water.

Identify blindfold the source of running water. Describe the direction and amount of the water.

Analyse sounds made by water when it is poured over different substances at different speeds and in different amounts.

Water in nature.

Study of rivers, streams, lakes and the sea.

Water storage.

How is water stored and purified?

Origins of water.

Study of rain-water, the water cycle, etc.

Projects on things around us: Travel (AT3: Earth and environment) (AT5: Energy and its effects)

Investigate use of headlights, torches and other lights in the dark.

Travelling by day and night.

Which objects allow light to travel through them and which do not?

Travelling light.

Experiment with releasing air from balloons to demonstrate the principles of rocket movement. Does the shape of the balloon have any effect on its movement?

Rockets.

TRAVEL

Test ways of blocking out traffic noises – with closed doors and windows, etc. Which ways are the most effective?

Noise pollution.

Experiments with echoes.

Travelling sound.

How the Earth travels through the solar system.

Use torch and rotating globe to explain how the movement of the Earth around the Sun gives us day and night.

Projects on things around us: Weather (AT3: Earth and environment) (AT5: Energy and its effects)

Show how plants need light in order to grow.

Experiment with sunlight bouncing off mirrors and glass. Study reflections.

The sun.

Wind.

Use the weather vane as a springboard for work on the points of the compass.

What noise does the wind make? Does the noise change when there is more or less wind? What is the wind?

Make a windsock and a weather vane.

Listen for the sound of thunder. Make a study of clouds and rain.

WEATHER

The sounds of weather.

Rain.

Study ways of keeping dry.

Collect and measure rainfall.

Examine changes in the sky before it rains.

Chapter Three
Cross-curricular projects

It is possible to include most of the timetabled subjects in cross-curricular projects. Although there will be some projects which do not seem to offer much scope for science work, sometimes it is easy to come up with projects which have a strong science element.

The projects covered in this chapter are 'Toys', 'Myself' and 'Hot and cold'. These offer a wide range of possibilities for work in many areas of the curriculum, and for each project there are listed a variety of activities relevant to the different curriculum areas.

Toys

Science

Movement

Make a collection of as many moving toys as you can. Ask the children to sort them out by the ways in which they move, and put them in lists of rolling toys, pulling toys, pushing toys, floating toys, flying toys, jumping toys, spinning toys and mechanical toys.

Can some of the toys be classified into more than one group? Encourage the children to examine all the toys and try to find out which are the moving parts in each one. How do these parts make the toys move? Which rolling toys roll furthest? What is there about this toy which makes it go further than the others? Let the children test the other toys in the same way, and find out what makes the best jumping toy jump further than the others, and so on.

Do the toys perform differently on different surfaces? Let the children try them out on a variety of surfaces, for example sloping, rough and slippery surfaces. Does the weight of the toy make any difference to the way in which it moves along these surfaces? Does the shape have any effect on movement? What do the children need to do to make a rolling toy start moving? How can they make it roll further, or faster? Ask them to make their own simple toys which roll, or which can be pulled or pushed, or which float, fly, jump or spin.

Balloons

Let the children blow up some balloons and take them outside on a windy day. Which way do the balloons go? What do the children think causes this? Let them fix small pieces of Plasticine to the nozzles of some balloons, and then release them into the wind. What difference do the pieces of Plasticine make to the speed at which the balloons go? What is the size of the smallest possible piece of Plasticine needed to stop the balloon soaring off altogether? What has this piece of Plasticine done to the balloon?

Take some balloons out on other occasions.

Ask the children to watch whether the balloons always fly off in the same direction. Can they find out the directions of the main compass points in the school playground?

Ask the children to form pairs and blow up a round balloon, using a pump. Tell them to stop after every two or three pumps. Can they think of a way of measuring the size of the balloon each time they stop pumping? Ask them to write down these measurements. Which are the smallest and largest measurements? Ask the children to compare their balloon's measurements with those of the rest of the class.

Design and technology

Stilts

Let the children design and make a pair of stilts out of two large, strong cans and some cord. What is the purpose of the stilts? What problems of movement do the children have to overcome when using the stilts? How can they ensure that the stilts are safe? How can they control them?

Games

Ask the children to try to design and make games from different pieces of waste material and litter. Make a catching game out of a large plastic bottle with a handle and a small square piece of wood. Cut the bottle in half and bore a hole through the wood. Ask the children to thread a long piece of string through the wood and tie the other end of the string to the handle of the bottle. Then they can hold the neck of the bottle and jerk the piece of wood into the air. Ask them to try to catch the piece of wood in the bottle.

How many times out of ten can the children do this? What makes the piece of wood fly into the air? What makes it come down again? Let them make up some rules for the game and give it an interesting name. Ask them to decorate the toy. Let them compete to see who is the best at the game, and then ask the children to make graphs and charts to show their scores.

What other games can they make out of litter? Can they develop a game of skittles out of plastic bottles? Can they make a set of draughts out of bottle tops? What skills do they need to play the games they invent?

Mathematics

Measurements

With a watch, the children should measure the time it takes for different toys to cover the same area of ground. They can use a ruler to measure the amount of space a wheeled toy takes to stop after it has rolled down a ramp. Ask the children to make graphs to show the results of these measurements.

Geography

Locations

Where in the town nearest the school can toys be purchased? Encourage the children to make a map showing the ways to the different toy shops.

History

Old toys

Ask the children to bring to school toys that their parents or grandparents played with when they were young. How do these differ from the toys the children have today? Are modern toys more mechanical? Are they better designed? Why do the children think that the toys their parents and grandparents played with are a little simpler than some of the toys they play with today? See if the children can design a toy which a child might play with in a hundred years' time.

Art

Pictures

Let the children make pictures of their favourite toys, using a variety of techniques. Perhaps they could make a picture from torn paper pasted on to dark sugar paper. Then they could try pasting coloured paper on to white paper. Finally, let them make a collage of old postage stamps or cut-out pictures pasted on to coloured pastel paper cut into the shapes of toys.

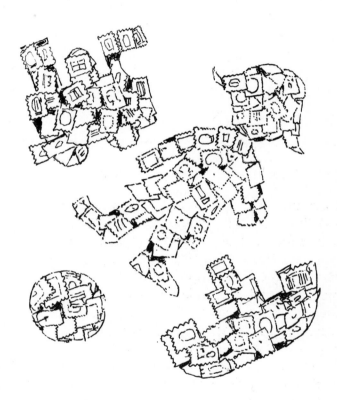

English

Literature

Read to the children *Pinocchio* by C Collodi (Ladybird) and *Thomas the Tank Engine* by Rev W Awdry (Kaye and Ward).
 Read the following poem:

Toy Shop
What have I got in my toy shop today,
Toy shop today, toy shop today;
What have I got in my top shop today?
You tell me.

Anon

Talking

Ask the children in turn to talk about the first toys they owned. Did they have a favourite? What was it? How long did they keep it? Where is it now?

Organise them into pairs so that one child takes on the role of the toy, and the other that of the owner. Let the 'toy' tell the 'owner' what she likes and dislikes about life. The 'toy' should imagine that she is:

● a teddy bear,
● a jack-in-the-box,
● a toy elephant,
● an old glove puppet.

Writing

Ask the children to make up and write a short play in which a number of toys come to life and go off on an adventure. Alternatively, let them write about a talking doll who loses her voice. She goes to the other toys and asks how she can get her voice back. What do the other toys say to her?

Music

Singing

Sing with the children 'The Teddy Bears' Picnic' (Bratton/Kennedy).

Myself

Science

Movements

Let the children move each part of their bodies in turn, and ask them to write down the name of each part they have moved. Under the heading 'Moving parts', ask each child to draw a picture of her body and write down in the correct place the name of each part which she can move. How many different ways can the children move each part of their bodies? What can they do with their arms, legs, wrists and hands, ankles and feet, waist, neck and head? Can the same things be done with one arm, one leg and one hand as can be done with two of each? Let them experiment and find out for themselves. How have they used the different parts of their bodies in the past? Ask them to write about the greatest distance they have ever walked, run, jumped, cycled or swum. For each of these activities, what combination of the parts of the body did they use? See how many different kinds of movement they can make with one partner, two partners, and the rest of the class.

Senses

Discuss with the children how difficult life is when one or more of the senses are not functioning properly. Let them write about what it feels like to operate without the full use of a particular sense.

Let them find out how it feels to perform various simple tasks:
- Put a simple jigsaw together while blindfolded, with only a partner to tell where the different pieces are and what they look like,
- Put a simple construction kit together while wearing thick, heavy gloves,
- Pinch the nostrils together with a peg and breathe through the mouth while trying to identify a number of different smells,
- Put cotton wool in the ears while blindfolded.

Ask them to identify the noises being made by other children, and say where these noises come from.

Let the children eat three or four very strong peppermints, and then give them a variety of foods and drinks to identify.

Organise the children into groups. Let each child in turn talk to the others in the group about what it was like trying to operate without the full use of the senses.

Discuss with the children how people with sense impairment manage, and the types of equipment which help them. Talk about the different types of hearing aids for deaf people, the reading system for the blind which is called Braille, and so on.

Appearance

Ask each child what he looks like. Make a chart for each child and let the children give details about their appearance:

Name	
Age	
Sex	
Colour of hair	
Colour of eyes	
Height	
Chest measurement	
Waist measurement	
Weight.	

Ask them to design and make their own passports giving these details. They could bring in a photograph of themselves to stick into the passport or draw a self-portrait. Let the children compare the details on their passports. A series of charts could be made to show the children with fair hair, with dark hair, with brown hair and with red hair, and so on. Let the children interview each other to find out more details. The interviewees could be asked about their favourite foods and drinks, the time they go to bed at night, their hobbies and so on.

Design and technology

Helping
After the personal details and measurements of the children have been worked out, see whether they can decide what they might need to help them, and let them try to design and make these objects. How can the smallest child in the class see over the heads of the others from the back of a crowd? Can they design and make something that he can carry around easily, which is safe to operate? Can they design and make something which will help the weaker children to pick up heavy objects, perhaps using a lever?

Mathematics

Graphs
Using the details of the measurements, habits, likes and dislikes of the children in the class, make some graphs to show various patterns such as the ages of the children from the youngest to the oldest, their heights from shortest to tallest, their weights from lightest to heaviest, their chest and waist measurements from smallest to largest.

Is there any obvious correlation to be found in these charts? Are the heavier children slower runners than the lighter ones on the whole? Are the lighter children generally weaker than the heavier ones? (Take care not to let anyone feel inferior.)

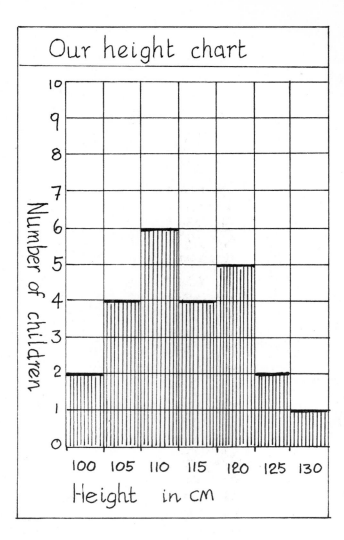

Geography

Children around the world
Make a study of children around the world and see how they compare with the class. Are their homes the same? Do they eat the same food? Is the climate different in various parts of the world? What are their schools like? Do they wear the same kinds of clothes as the class?

History

Jobs
Discuss how, in the past, children had to go out and work when they were little older than the children in the class. Some worked as chimney-sweeps, climbing up chimneys to clean them; others worked in coal-mines. In some countries, children still have to work.

Art

Friends

Ask the children to draw pictures of several of their friends, using different techniques. They could draw a silhouette, drawing round the shadow of one child as she sits in the dark in front of a white screen with a torch shining on her head. Let them draw an outline of the whole head and body and stick pieces of fabric on to the outline to make a fabric portrait.

English

Literature

Read to the class a variety of stories about toys; try *Stories for Six-Year-Olds* and *Stories for Seven-Year-Olds*, both by Sara and Stephen Corrin (Faber and Faber).

Read the followng poems:

Johnny Head-in-Air

As he trudged along to school,
It was always Johnny's rule
To be looking at the sky
And the clouds that floated by;
But what just before him lay,
In his way,
Johnny never thought about;
So that everyone cried out:
"Look at little Johnny there,
Little Johnny Head-in-Air!"

Heinrich Hoffman

and;

Shut the Door

Godfrey Gordon Gustavus Gore-
No doubt you've heard the name before-
Was a boy who never would shut a door!

The wind might whistle, the wind might
roar,
And teeth be aching, and throats be sore,
But still he never would shut the door.

William Brighty Rands

Talking

Have the children prepare a two-minute talk about themselves, and ask each child to deliver it to the rest of the class.

This can be followed by a two-minute talk about 'Your best friend'.

Writing

Ask the children the following questions and let them write down their answers. What is it like to be you? What can you remember about your life before you came to school? What is the best story you have ever read about a young child? What did you like about it?

Have them make a book entitled *Myself*. They could put in it everything they think is of interest; things they have done, things they have seen, their favourite poems, and so on.

Music

Singing

Sing with the children 'Here We Go Looby Loo' (Anon).

Hot and cold

Science

Making heat

Ask the children to make a list of all the cold places in the school, and then a list of the warm or hot places. What can they use to find the temperatures of these places? How could the cold places be made warmer? In the course of a day, how many objects can they find which would help warm them up? What forms of heating are there at home and at school?

Can they find gas fires, electric fires and oil-fired radiators? What are the temperatures close to these heaters? Does the temperature fall the further away they are from each heater, or does it remain the same? Which type of heating is the best?

Ask the children to rub their hands together hard. How do they begin to feel? What happens the harder they rub their hands together? What other things can be warmed like this?

Take a piece of sandpaper and some wood. Sandpaper the wood for several minutes. Then let the children feel the sandpaper and the wood. How do they seem now? What changes have taken place? Let the children rub more things together and record the results. They could try with two pieces of wood, two pieces of metal and two stones. The children may find that if they rub certain things together hard enough something may be produced. Can they tell what it is? What does this have to do with heat? Explain that when two objects are rubbed together, tiny particles called molecules inside the objects are disturbed. They shake, or vibrate, and make heat.

drinks cool before drinking them? Do they taste as good now? Which drinks are just as pleasant hot as cold? At what time of the year do most people prefer hot drinks? When is it best to have cold drinks?

Put one teabag in a glass of cold water and another in a glass of hot water. In which glass does the water turn brown first? Put two more teabags in glasses of cold water. Leave one alone and stir the other. Which one turns brown first? What happens when the water is stirred? Among other things, the molecules in the water have been disturbed. What effect would that have had on the teabag in the water?

Heating liquids

Have the children make a list of all the cold drinks that they like. Then ask them to make a list of hot drinks, like chocolate or milk.

Let them collect together as many drinks as they can and examine them. What difference does it make if some of the cold drinks are heated? Does it improve or spoil their taste? What happens if they let some of the hot

Heating air

Turn on a hair-drier and let the children feel the air coming out. What happens to this air after a minute or two? What has it become? What has caused this? Pump a bicycle pump into the air. Does the air coming out of the pump change at all after a time? Show the children what happens to a paper bag if it is held over a candle, thus heating the air inside it. Do not allow the children to try this experiment unsupervised.

Design and technology

Hot-water bottle
Let the children design a cover for a hot-water bottle which will be attractive to look at, will slip on and off the bottle easily and will hold the heat in the bottle. They should consider the best shape and material for the cover.

Mathematics

Temperatures
Show the children how to take their own temperature, and ask them to take it hourly in order to see if it changes during the day.

Does their temperature change after a games lesson or after they have been rushing around at playtime? Let them compare temperatures, and make a graph to show the temperatures of different children in the class at one point during the day.

Geography

Hot and cold lands
Compare the lives of children in hot and cold lands around the world. What would be the main differences in the life of a child living in Alaska and another living in Egypt? What differences would there be in their clothing, homes and food? Can the children think of other ways in which the climate influences the way we live?

History

Cold spells
Invite someone from the town or village to come and talk to the class about a particularly cold winter in the past. What happened to the rivers and ponds? How did the cold affect people's lives at the time? What could they do about the cold?

Art

Winter scenes

Make a number of pictures on the theme of winter, using different techniques. Show the children how to make a finger painting by brushing cold-water paste thickly over paper, and sprinkle powder paint on to the pasted surface before drawing a picture with their fingers.

They could try to make a similar picture using soap and powdered paint. Do this by putting a tablespoonful of soap powder in a jar and then adding a dessertspoonful of powdered paint. Stir the mixture together and paint on to a manila board.

English

Literature

Read *Summer in Small Street* by Geraldine Kaye (Mammoth) and *Father Christmas* by Raymond Briggs (Hamish Hamilton).

Discuss poems such as

<u>The Months</u>
January cold desolate,
February all dripping wet;
March wind ranges;
April changes;
Birds sing in tune
To flowers of May,
And sunny June
Brings longest day . . .

Christina Rossetti

and;

<u>The Robin</u>
When winter frost
Makes earth as steel,
I search and search
But find no meal,
And most unhappy
Then I feel.

Thomas Hardy

Talking

Encourage the children to imagine that they are making a radio broadcast about a dreadful snowstorm. They have to tell listeners what is happening and what everything looks like.

Ask the children to form pairs and pretend that they are Inuit, and that one of the pair has just built a house of snow and is now trying to sell it to the other. The seller has to show the potential buyer around the snow house, pointing out the good points and trying to persuade him to buy it.

Writing

Let the children consider the following ideas:
● You have built a spaceship that will take people to the sun. Write an advertisement to persuade people to come on board.
● You are a snowman, and you do not like it. Write a letter to the person who made you, telling her where she has gone wrong in the design. Tell your maker how you would like to be redesigned.

Music

Singing

Sing with the children 'I do Like to be Beside the Seaside' (Glover-Kind).

Chapter four
Delivering the attainment targets

The original attainment targets for science were:

AT1: Exploration of science
AT2: The variety of life
AT3: Processes of life
AT4: Genetics and evolution
AT5: Human influences on the Earth
AT6: Types and uses of materials
AT7: Making new materials
AT8: Explaining how materials behave
AT9: Earth and atmosphere
AT10: Forces
AT11: Electricity and magnetism
AT12: The scientific aspects of information technology including microelectronics
AT13: Energy
AT14: Sound and music
AT15: Using light and electromagnetic radiation
AT16: The Earth in space
AT17: The nature of science

These have now been superseded by the new attainment targets:

AT1: Scientific investigation
AT2: Life and living processes
AT3: Earth and environment
AT4: Materials and their behaviour
AT5: Energy and its effects

The children should continue their study of wildlife at first hand and through books, videos and television programmes. They should develop their understanding of the ways of looking after living things, and put this understanding into practice.

Level 3

Take the children to see plants in a range of natural habitats. Ask them to make lists of plants which grow in dry places, in wet places, in the sun and in the shade.

Encourage the children to compare these different plants. Do the plants growing in the shade have common characteristics? Do the plants which grow in wet places differ from those growing in dry areas?

Comparing plants

What you need
A variety of roots and plant stems, water, containers.

What to do
In order to help the children recognise similarities and differences among living things, let them make a collection of different roots. The children should examine the roots carefully, washing them and sorting them into two groups: fibrous roots, which look like clumps of thread; and tap-roots, which have larger main roots with side branches. Are any of these roots swollen because they are storing food? Can we eat any of them?

Ask the children to compare the lengths of the roots they have collected. How long is the longest? Are fibrous roots generally longer or shorter than tap-roots, or is there no obvious pattern?

Let the children make a collection of different plant stems, keeping them in water. How many are hollow? How long is the longest stem? Are round stems generally longer or shorter than square stems, or is there no discernable pattern?

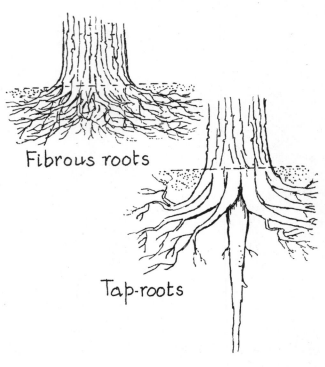

Types of roots

Fibrous roots

Tap-roots

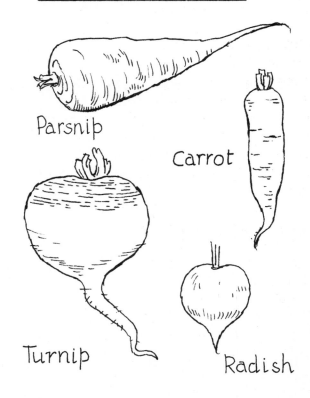

Some edible roots

Parsnip

Carrot

Turnip

Radish

72

Sorting seeds
What you need
An assortment of seeds, fruit stones and pips, bird seed, a variety of nuts.

What to do
Spend some time looking at different ways of sorting things. Let the children collect different varieties of seeds, and sort them by shape and then by size. They can then try to classify the seeds according to the different ways in which they are spread — falling to the ground, scattered by the wind, carried by animals, and so on.

The children could classify a variety of different fruit stones and pips by size, shape and texture. They could use the same classifications to sort the contents of a bag of mixed nuts.

During the winter, let the children put three or four different kinds of bird seed out on a bird table for a week. Which seeds do the birds seem to like most and least? Does the price of the bird seed have any bearing on the quality and popularity of the seed?

Levels 4 and 5

Soil and decay
What you need
A variety of soils, saucers, adhesive labels, pencils.

What to do
Combine work on the processes of decay with a study of how differences between locations are reflected in the number and variety of plant and animal species found.

Collect different kinds of soil. Put each sample in a different saucer and label each with its location. The darker soils may contain humus, which is made up of the rotting parts of animals and plants. It provides food for plants growing in the soil.

Go back with the children to where you found the dark soil. Does the soil there seem richer? Do more plants grow there than in other areas? If so, can the children see why this might be?

Plants and soil

What you need

Small tin, soil, scissors, basin, water, large jar, tin plate, weighing scales, pencils, paper, glass-sided case.

What to do

● In order to see how much air there is in soil, first knock some holes in the bottom of a small tin, and fill the tin with soil. Find a jar large enough to go over the tin, and fill the jar with water. Cover the top of the jar with a tin plate, and holding the plate in place, very carefully turn the jar upside down. Place it, still upside down, in a basin of water. Now remove the tin plate from under the jar, and without lifting the jar above the water, place the tin of soil beneath the jar, with the holes uppermost. Ask the children to watch what comes out of the holes. Can they see what this means?

● To see how much water there is in soil, first weigh some soil and write down the weight. Then put the soil in a tin, and bake it in the oven at a low temperature for about three hours. Now empty the soil on to a set of scales and record the weight. Ask the children if they can guess what causes the difference in the weight before and after baking the soil. What has been removed from the soil in the baking process?

● In order to see how the roots of a plant seek out the water the plant needs, let the children plant some seeds in a glass-sided case. They should water the seeds until the roots begin to grow, and then stop watering the soil directly above the seeds, moistening the area a little to one side of the roots instead. What do the roots do?

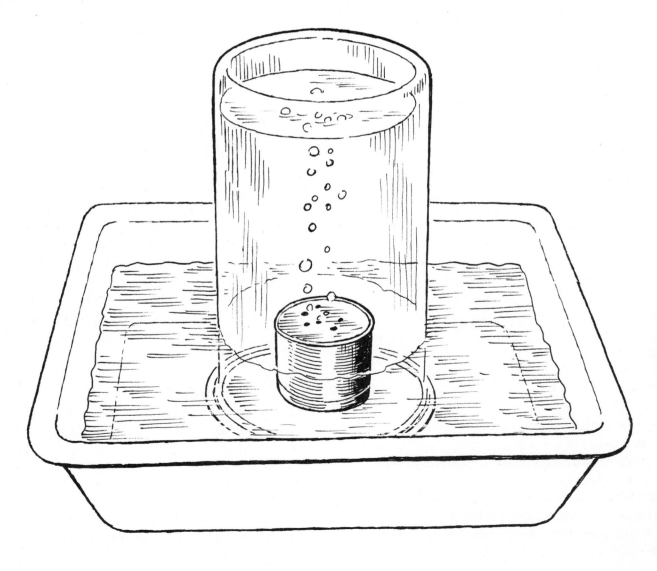

Plants and fertilizers

What you need
Collection of ferns, lichens and mosses, packet of seeds, tubs, fertilizer or plant food.

What to do
Introduce the children to the use of fertilizers on the soil. First of all, bring in some plants such as lichens, ferns and mosses, which need little or no soil in which to grow. Ask the children to compare these with some plants grown in soil. How do they compare in size and luxuriance of growth?

In a patch of the school garden, or in a couple of tubs in the classroom, plant in soil two lots of identical seeds. Water both sets of seeds, but use fertilizers on one only. Ask the children to compare the rates of growth.

Investigate the side-effects of using fertilizers; the harmful effects as well as the good ones.

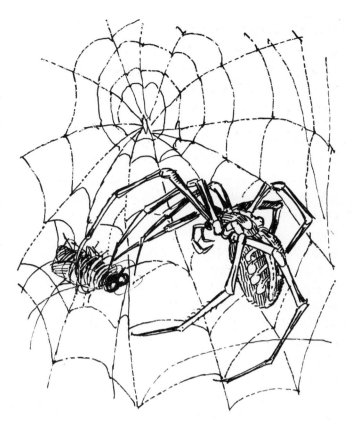

Predators

What you need
Spider's web, pencils, paper.

What to do
In order to introduce the children to the topic of predators and prey, find a spider's web near the classroom and ask the children to keep a diary of the way it is used by the spider. They can then use this as the basis of an investigation into the ways in which creatures prey on one another. How do human beings prey? What animals do not prey on others? How do these survive?

Fossilization

What you need
Collection of fossils, paper, pencils.

What to do
Perhaps the best way of putting over the idea that plants and animals may be preserved as fossils is to let the children make a class collection of different sorts of fossils. Encourage them to try to identify and classify the fossils.

Information technology

Use a variety of instruments (including barometers, thermometers and wind-gauges) to detect changes in the environment, and study the effects these have on living things.

Cross-curricular activities

● Encourage the children to read books about wildlife and plants, including perhaps *Over the Steamy Swamp* by Paul Geraghty (Hutchinson) and *Fantastic Mr Fox* by Roald Dahl (Puffin).
● Use the theme of predators and prey in a history project such as the invasions of Britain by the Romans, Anglo-Saxons and Vikings.
● Make bark rubbings on thick paper. Cut these out in the shapes of tree trunks and stick them to the walls of the classroom. Collect leaves from all sorts of trees. Paste these leaves on to the trunks made from bark rubbings to make a 'wood' in the classroom.
● Make pictures by sticking flat seeds on stiff cards.

Summary

● Differences in location can have a tremendous effect on growing things.
● Decaying matter can affect the soil.
● Characteristics of decay are an increase in temperature, the presence of microbes, compactness and moisture.
● Soil is made up of particles of rock, sand, clay and the remains of plants and animals.
● Plants cannot move in search of food. Some of them store food in their swollen parts, such as the leaves, stems and roots.

The children should be encouraged to study a wide variety of living things in order to understand that the basic life processes are common to all animals, including human beings.

Level 3

Keeping fit
What you need
Pencils, paper.

What to do
Without over-straining any child, compare the basic standards of physical prowess in the class. Explain to the children the importance of regular exercise and keeping fit. Get each child in turn to crouch and stand again. How many times can the children do this before they become tired? How long can the children hold their arms extended sideways? Do the same children get the best results each time? Is there any connection between the size of a child and his strength? Use the results of these studies for a series of graphs, diagrams and wall-charts.

The human body
What you need
Paper, large bottle with screw-top lid, rubber tubing, tray, jars for measuring, marbles.

What to do
The physical activities described in 'Keeping fit' can be used as the basis for a study of the main functions of the human body.
● Study the workings of the heart and bloodstream by showing how the heart acts as a pump. Tie a taper or spill to the wrist of each child just where the thumb begins; there is an artery at this point. The taper should jerk every time the child's heart beats. Get the children to count how many times their hearts beat in a minute, and to record and compare their results.
● As an introduction to the functions of the lungs, see how much air each child can take into her lungs. Obtain a large bottle with a screw-top lid, one long and one short piece of rubber tubing, a tray and some measuring jars. Bore two holes in the lid of the bottle. Place a piece of tubing through each hole. Fill the

bottle with water, screw on the top and place the bottle on its side in a container or tray. Ask each child in turn to blow into the long rubber tube. This will force water out of the bottle, through the shorter tube and into the tray. The child should keep blowing until her lungs are empty. Pour the water from the tray and measure it in one of the jars. The water will have the same capacity as the air blown out of the child's lungs.

Which child has the greatest lung capacity and which has the smallest? Can the children see any correlation between lung capacity and the ability to run fast? Ask them to make charts, graphs and diagrams to compare the lung capacities of different children.

● The digestive system's workings can be included in a general project on food. In order to demonstrate how the muscles of the stomach squeeze food through the digestive tract, ask each child to squeeze a marble through a tube from one end to the other. Explain how the body extracts goodness from food and passes out waste.

Level 4

Reproduction

What you need
Pictures and videos of mammals and their young, piece of meat, jar, fly.

What to do
A basic study of reproduction in mammals could be used as part of the school sex education policy, and should be preceded by the use of pictures, videos and television programmes showing the children how young mammals resemble their parents and grow to look and act like them.

● Encourage the children to study examples of the reproduction of insects. Put a small piece of meat and a piece of paper soaked in water in a glass jar. Catch a fly and place it in the jar. Put the lid on the jar. Observe what happens on the meat as the fly lays eggs, and as the eggs develop through all the stages to become adult flies.

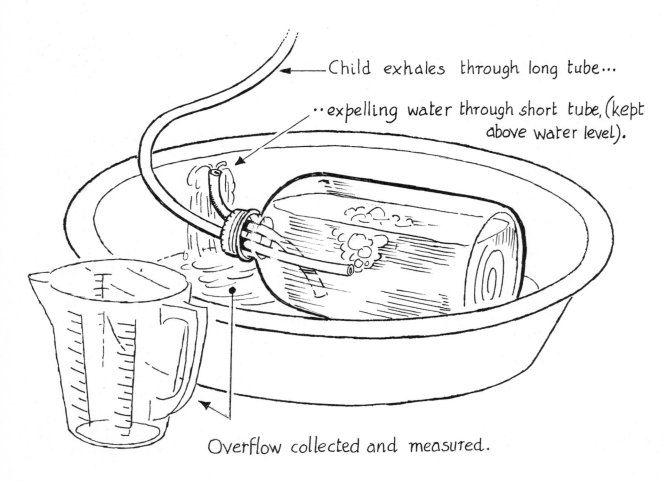

Child exhales through long tube...

..expelling water through short tube, (kept above water level).

Overflow collected and measured.

The growth of moulds

What you need
Pieces of cheese, pencils, paper.

What to do
Emphasise the importance of storing and handling food correctly to prevent moulds.

Place a piece of cheese in the sun, another piece in a cool, shady place, and a third piece of cheese in a refrigerator. Observe and measure the growth of the moulds on each piece of cheese. Which cheese lasts the longest without growing a mould? How can we use this information in order to preserve food?

Major organs of plants

What you need
Assortment of plants and flowers, soil, water, craft knife, two potted plants.

What to do
Show the children how the roots anchor a plant in the soil by taking a plant and cutting off the roots, leaving the stem. Ask the children to stand the stem upright on some soil. What happens? How would the roots have helped had they been left in place?

● Have the children push the stem into the soil so that the plant stands upright. Let them water the plant and look after it for a week. What happens to it? What might have happened had the roots still been attached? What would the function of the roots have been in this case?

● Next, show how the stems carry water and minerals from the roots to the rest of the plant. Cut open a number of stems of different plants. What is inside them? What does this mean? Are the interiors of all the stems the same?

● Study how leaves make food for plants. Take two similar potted plants, and remove the leaves from one of them. Look after both plants in exactly the same way for a week, placing them in sunlight and watering them regularly. After a week, what is the difference between the two plants? Can the children guess what causes the difference? What does this mean?

● Study the reproduction of flowering plants. Ask the children to pick flowers from a number of plants and examine their seeds. How do they differ and in what ways are they the same? Encourage the children to try to find out how the seeds are dispersed.

Level 5

Cell structure

What you need

Onion, iodine, glass slide, microscope.

What to do

The children should now be ready to undertake a more theoretical study of cells. A cell is the smallest unit of life which can exist independently. Let the children examine this by taking a single tissue from an onion. They should put the tissue in a drop of water on a glass slide, and place a drop of iodine on the tissue. Then they can observe the cells through a microscope. Ask them to make a diagram of the ways in which the cells are arranged. You could use this work to help explain that all living things are made up of cells.

Me by Sally Christie and Peter Kavanagh (Black/Collins).
● Include in a history project a study of how youths in ancient Greece were encouraged to develop their bodies and become athletes.
● The reproduction of flowers could be included in the school's sex education policy. Flowers are involved in sexual reproduction. The stamen is the male part. The pistil is the female part, comprising a pollen-receiving stigma, a style and an ovary, which bears the embryo seed or ovule. Pollen grains are transferred by the wind or by insects like bees.

Function of the skin
What you need
One rotten apple and one in good condition.

What to do
Study the function of the skin as part of a health and hygiene project. Our skin protects us from tiny organisms, which could harm our bodies.

Compare a rotten apple with one in good condition. What happens to the good apple if it is bruised by being hurled to the floor and a small incision is made in its skin? What does this tell us about looking after our skin and bodies?

Information technology
● Use videos and computer games to demonstrate the functions of the heart, lungs and other organs, and to show the parts of a plant and their functions.

Cross-curricular activities
● Introduce the children to books which will help them in their understanding of the functions of the human body. These could include *Before You Were Born* by Margaret Sheffield and Sheila Bewley (Cape) and *Weedy*

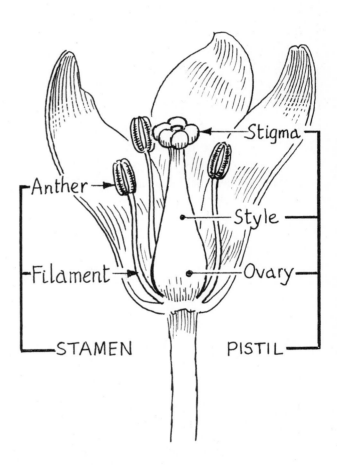

Summary
● Food provides us with energy. It is digested in the body and enters the bloodstream.
● The heart pumps blood around the body.
● In the lungs the blood is enriched with oxygen, which is breathed in with the air.
● Poisonous carbon dioxide is pushed out of the body by the lungs when we breathe out.

This target could be linked with various history projects, as it concentrates on the study of extinct forms of life and on the passing on of information from one generation to the next through genes, as well as on similarities and differences between living things.

Level 3

Let the children study the living history of the area. What historical landmarks are there? Are there any war memorials or other records of the past? Can the children find out which periods they come from? Can they find any photographs or paintings of the area as it used to be?

Try to persuade some older members of the community to come in to the school and talk about the changes that have taken place in the district during their lifetimes.

Effects of time on objects
What you need
Pieces of coal, bowls of water, fossils, leaves, Plasticine, cardboard, plaster of Paris, plastic trays, blackberries or cherries.

What to do
Obtain pieces of coal and bowls of water. Tell the children that the coal we use is made up of leaves and plants and some of it may be 300 million years old. Some of the water we drink has been on earth long enough to have been drunk by dinosaurs in prehistoric times.

Show the children a collection of fossils, and explain that these were made in a variety of ways. For example, the shells of sea creatures left their imprints in rock when more rock pressed down on top of them over a period of thousands of years.

● Ask the children to make their own model fossils. Place a leaf on a flat piece of Plasticine.

Embed a tube of cardboard in the Plasticine around the leaf. Pour a thin paste of plaster of Paris over the leaf inside the cardboard tube. When the plaster has set, take away the Plasticine and the cardboard. Ask the children to compare their fossils.

● Put some fruits like blackberries or cherries in a tray of water on a classroom shelf. Put some more blackberries or cherries in a tray of water in the freezer compartment of a refrigerator. Which fruits are preserved the longest? Can the children see what this has to do with preserving the bodies of animals long dead? Where would they expect to find these preserved remains?

Level 4

Differences between living organisms
What you need
Assortment of animal leg bones.

What to do
Let the children make a collection of the leg bones of different animals. Ask them to compare the bones in terms of length and weight. Can they think of other criteria for comparing the bones?

Recording children's differences
What you need
Pencils, paper, ball.

What to do
Measure and record the heights of all the children in the class. Measure them again six months later, and then after a year. Who has gained the most and who has gained the least? Ask the children to make a similar comparison of gains in weight during this period.

Ask the children to work out which muscles or combinations of muscles are used for various tasks such as lifting a weight, kicking a ball and pushing a trolley. Can all the children perform these activities with equal ease?

Level 5

Inheritance
What you need
No special equipment.

What to do
Hold an investigation to see if children inherit particular physical attributes from their parents. Do the children generally have the same colour eyes and hair as their parents? Can they think of any other attributes they might have inherited from their parents? This investigation could be used to introduce the idea that information in the form of genes is passed on from one generation to the next.

Information technology
Use films and videos to show the children how people used to live in the past. Encourage the children to compare and contrast these ways of life with our own.

Cross-curricular activities
● The children should be encouraged to read works of fiction which bring the past to life, such as *The Eagle of the Ninth* by Rosemary Sutcliffe (Puffin), *Silver's Revenge* by Robert Leeson (Collins) and *Keeping Henry* by Nina Bawden (Puffin).
● Make a frieze in the form of a time-chart, showing aspects of local history.
● Use a study of evolution as the basis for a moral education study of racial equality and tolerance, showing how our early ancestors adapted to different climates in various ways; for example, some developed dark skins to absorb some of the sun's radiation. This study could be linked with an examination of the many languages of mankind.

Summary
● Some forms of life became extinct recently, while other forms became extinct long ago.
● We can still trace forms of life which no longer exist. We call these fossils.
● Through their genes, people can pass on certain physical attributes to their children and their children's children and so on.

At this level the children should be encouraged to take an interest in and appreciate their environment, and to recognize the changes being made in it, for good and ill, by people.

Level 3

Examine the effects of human activities on the landscape near the school. Go with the children to look at tunnels, roads and bridges. Which signs of human activity seem good and which seem harmful?

Encourage the children to get involved in a supervised community activity helping to look after the environment – perhaps clearing a footpath, or cleaning a church-yard. Ask them to write about the results of their activities, and to draw maps, diagrams and graphs to show the project's progress.

Water and pollution
What you need
Water from different sources, funnel, blotting paper, jar, saucers.

What to do
Collect a number of examples of polluted water from the vicinity. Show the children how to make a filter by lining a funnel with blotting paper. Place the funnel in an empty jar, and pour the water into it. Ask the children to notice and record what happens as the water works its way into the jar. Make the point that when water has been cleaned scientifically it can be used again – water can be recycled. Where does the dirtiest water in the area come from? Is anything being done to clean it?

Let the children repeat this experiment using a number of different filters: gravel, different kinds of cloth and so on. Which of the filters they devise is the most effective? Why do they think this is?

Make a study of the water coming through the taps in the children's homes. Ask each of them to bring to school a sample of their tap water. Put each sample in a different saucer. Place the saucers in the sun until the water has evaporated. When there is no water left, let the children examine the saucers. Are there any white marks on the sides or bottom? If so, these will be the remains of solids which were once in the water. Which saucer has the fewest marks and which has the most? Compare the saucers according to streets and areas.

Litter
What you need
Classroom rubbish, paper sacks, weighing scales.

What to do
For a week, let each class in the school put its rubbish in paper sacks rather than in bins and baskets. At the end of the week, let the children compare each class's litter. Ask them to weigh the litter produced by each class. Which class produces the most and which the least? Where does their own class come in this league table? Is there any correlation between the amount of rubbish produced and the number or ages of the children in a class? Add up the weight of the rubbish produced by a whole school. Can the children work out how much would be produced in 40 weeks, in ten years, in a hundred years? Ask them to find out how the school's rubbish is disposed of. Is any of it recycled? Could more be recycled?

Protect the environment
What you need
Paper sacks, brooms, large steel bin for a bottle bank, hammers, nails, planks of wood for a birdtable, pencils, paper.

What to do
Improve the environment through projects such as organizing a newspaper collection or bottle bank, developing a scheme for saving

energy in the school, keeping the school tidy, building a bird table or nesting box, and helping wildlife in the area. Ask the children to describe what was planned and what was achieved.

Level 4

Recycling
What you need
Old clothes, jars, paints, paintbrushes, detergent bottles, newspaper, milk-bottle tops.

What to do
A discussion on recycling should be prefaced by explaining and demonstrating that some waste products do not deteriorate and may be used again.

Among the recycling projects which could be undertaken are making a rag doll out of old clothes, making a papier mâché model from old newspapers, decorating jars and using them to store things in, making a pencil case from an old detergent bottle, and using milk-bottle tops as 'armour' in a frieze of knights in battle.

Level 5

The growth of moulds
What you need
Towel, small cloths, foodstuffs such as slices of bread, cheese, jam and milk, plastic dishes.

What to do
Show the class that some microbes such as mould and bacteria are harmful; let them see how easy it is for microbes to grow. Place a wet towel in a dark place for a week. Then look at it. There should be a number of dark spots of mildew on the towel. Mildew is a mould, upon which bacteria can grow.

Moulds grow more quickly in hot places than cold ones. Put a wet cloth in a warm, damp cupboard. Place another wet cloth on a desk. Put a third wet cloth in a refrigerator. At the end of a week, examine all three cloths for moulds. What do the children notice?

Let the childen watch the growth of moulds on different foods. Put out a selection of foods on saucers – moist bread, cheese, jam and milk. Cover each saucer with a plastic dish. Ask the children to make notes about what happens each day, and describe the moulds that grow. They can compare the different moulds as they change shape.

Preventing decay
What you need
Pieces of cheese, dried foods such as cereals and dried fruit, salt, water, cucumber, dishes.

What to do
Once the children have grasped the concept that some microbes can be spoiling agents, let them undertake some activities which show that there are ways of preventing harmful microbes spoiling the food we eat.

Microbes need warmth to grow. Put one piece of cheese on a table and one in a refrigerator. Which grows mould first?

Microbres need moisture in order to grow. If moisture is absent microbes will grow only slowly, if at all. Collect some dried foods such as cereals and dried fruit. How long is it before microbes grow on them?

Microbes cannot grow easily in sugar or salt. Make a mixture of salt and water (brine). Put several pieces of sliced cucumber in a container of brine. Place several more pieces of cucumber in a container without brine. After a week, let the children examine the differences between the two samples of cucumber. What has happened? What does this mean?

Explain that some waste products are biodegradable – that is, they can be changed by the influence of microbes. Other waste products cannot be changed by the workings of microbes; these are non-biodegradable.

Biodegradable and non-biodegradable
What you need
Scraps of wood, foodstuffs, china, plastic containers, newspapers, gloves.

What to do
Wearing gloves and observing safety precautions, make a collection of a number of waste products, including pieces of wood, china, plastic, food and paper. Leave them all outside for a week or so. Which of them seem to be changing under the influence of microbes and which do not? Make two lists; one of biodegradable objects and the other of non-biodegradable objects.

Improving the environment

What you need
Pencils, paper, equipment for model-making.

What to do
Ask the children to decide on one major environmental problem area in the vicinity of the school. What could be done to improve it? Let them make notes and models, using the information gathered, to show how this area could be made better. Invite someone from a local conservation group to come in to the school and talk about it.

Information technology

• Show the children how to make a simple microscope. Twist a wire until one end forms a loop about 2 mm across. Wipe some grease around the edges of the loop. Dip the loop into a glass of water and withdraw it. A drop of water should then be stretched across the loop. This is a microscope. Hold the microscope over the pages of a book. What happens? Ask the children to write about what they see, and then hold the microscope over a number of other small objects and write about what happens.
• Use a real microscope to examine insects, some Epsom salts, a piece of cheese, etc. Ask the children to describe what they see.

Cross-curricular activities

• Introduce the children to books about our endangered planet and the efforts being made to help it. Fiction on this general theme includes any of the books about the Wombles by Elizabeth Beresford (Puffin), *Who Ever Heard of a Vegetarian Fox?* by Rosalind Kerven (Blackie/Puffin) and *Mrs Frisby and the Rats of NIMH* by Robert C. O'Brien (Gollancz/Puffin).
• Link a study of bacteria and microbes with the development of food storage facilities at sea over the ages, and attempts by early seafarers to avoid scurvy.
• Encourage the children to use recycled objects in their craft work. They could try making a candle holder by putting a candle stuck in Plasticine in the bottom of a decorated jar, or threading drink cans together on long strings and painting and decorating them to look like serpents.

Summary

• Our Earth is always changing, not always for the better. Among the dangers faced by our planet are pollution, the accumulation of waste and the erosion of arable land.
• Disease may be spread by microbes, which gather on rubbish.
• Bacteria are among the smallest of all living things. They are so tiny that the point of a needle will cover hundreds.
• Some bacteria are useful; they help make cheese and yoghurt. Some are used in making medicines such as antibiotics. Some bacteria help break things up and get rid of waste.
• Some bacteria are harmful. They spoil our food and can sometimes enter our bodies and make us ill.

Let the children undertake activities which will help them understand that air is all around us, that wind is air in motion and that soil is caused by the weathering of rocks.

Level 3

Air is all around

What you need

Deflated football, air pump, ruler, newspaper, paper bag.

What to do

Ask the children to weigh a deflated football. Then they can pump it up until it is hard, and weigh it again. Is it heavier now that there is air inside it? What does this mean?

● To emphasise the fact that air has weight, even if it cannot be seen, place a ruler across the edge of a table, with half the ruler on the table and the other half jutting out over the edge. Spread an open newspaper over the part that is on the table. The newspaper is light. Strike the part of the ruler sticking out beyond the edge of the table. Does it lift the newspaper? If not, why not?

● Although we cannot see it, air takes up space. Blow up a paper bag and seal the end. Throw it as far as you can. Throw an empty paper bag in the same direction. Which goes furthest? What does this mean?

same inside and outside the bag. When the air was sucked out of the bag, the air pressure inside decreased and could not push the sides of the bag out as strongly. The pressure outside the bag continued to push inwards, making the bag crumple and fold.

● To help the children understand how strong the pressure of air can be, fill a bottle about three-quarters full of water. Put the top on the bottle, first having bored a hole through the top so that there is just enough space to insert a drinking straw. If there is any space around the straw, plug it with Plasticine. Blow steadily through the straw into the bottle. This will force more air into the bottle and force down or compress the air which is above the water in the bottle. Stop blowing suddenly, and stand back. Tell the children to watch the top of the straw. Does anything come out through it? What causes this?

Weathering of rocks and soil
What you need
Sedimentary rock, hammer, humus, compost, two pots, two plants of similar size and the same species, water, glass-sided case, earthworms, soil.

What to do
● To show that weathering of rocks causes different kinds of soil, find a piece of sedimentary rock, wrap it in a piece of cloth and hammer it into tiny pieces. Mix the minute particles of rock with humus and compost and put the mixture in a pot. Put some clayey or sandy soil in another pot. Select two similar plants, and plant one in each pot. Which grows quicker?

Explain to the children that normally the sedimentary rock would have needed many more years in which to disintegrate and mix with chemicals before becoming soil.

● Carry on the investigation of soil by half-filling a glass-sided container with soil and putting a number of earthworms in the container. Encourage the children to observe how the worms pass the soil through their bodies and make it finer.

Air pressure
What you need
Paper bags, bottle with top, drinking straw, Plasticine, craft knife, water.

What to do
Show that the pressure or force of air is the same in all directions. Ask the children to blow up an empty bag, and hold the neck of the bag tightly to keep the air in. Has the bag expanded? Then ask them to open the neck of the bag slightly and suck the air out. Does the bag crumple?

The bag remained expanded while the neck was closed because the air pressure was the

Level 4

Wind and rain
What you need
Stocking, length of wire, long pole, pencils, paper, measuring jar.

What to do
Show the children that wind is air in motion. Make a wind sock by cutting the toe off the end of a stocking and threading wire around the other end to hold it open. Attach this end of the stocking to a long pole, using another piece of wire. Plant the pole in the ground.

Every morning at the same time, ask the children to make a note of the direction from which the wind is coming. They should also note whether the wind is strong, moderate or weak. After a couple of weeks, they could make a chart, and draw some graphs and diagrams.
● Next, ask the children to make a wind-chart, with arms for each of the main compass points. They should mark off spaces for seven days on each of the arms of the chart, and each day they can colour in the appropriate square according to the direction that the wind is coming from.
● As well as recording the wind, the children could use a measuring jar to record the monthly, weekly or daily rainfall in the playground.

Climate and agriculture
What you need
Bucket.

What to do
Study the effects of climate on agriculture and on the growth of plants and crops.

Show the children that sunlight is essential for the healthy growth of plants. Light from the sun is absorbed by the green pigment chlorophyll, and used by the plant as a source of energy.

Put a bucket upside down over a patch of grass. After a week, remove the bucket. How does the grass beneath the bucket differ in

appearance from the rest of the grass? Can the children imagine what would happen to the crops on a farm if there was not enough sunlight? What would happen if there was not enough rainfall, or if there were too many storms?

Level 5

The weather cycle
What you need
Pencils, paper.

What to do
Complete the children's investigations into weather by asking them to draw and learn the weather cycle.

Explain that rain comes down from the clouds, but that a great deal of it goes back into the sky in the form of water vapour when the sun evaporates water in the seas and rivers. Ask the children to make a graph showing how many times it has rained each day during a week.

Formation of landscapes
What you need
Foam rubber sheeting of different colours.

What to do
Ask the children to make models of the surface of the Earth by sticking some foam rubber sheets of different colours on top of one another. Explain that each sheet represents a strata of rock, formed over a very long time. Explain how hills, valleys and other geological features are made by movements of the Earth's crust. Demonstrate this by pushing the foam rubber sheets together from different directions to make them buckle.

Information technology

Examine and use different kinds of barometer. Construct a barometer in class, to show the pressure of the air. Take a coffee tin with a plastic lid. Stick a straw across the top of the lid so that half of the straw is jutting out over the edge. Stick a pin to the end of the straw which juts out. Next to the tin, place upright a card upon which has been drawn a series of regularly spaced horizontal lines. Adjust the tin and the card so that the point of the pin is against the third line from the top of the card. Ask the children to observe the position of the pin every day for a month. Each day, record which line on the card it points to. Make a note of whether the point of the pin goes up or down. If the air pressure on top of the lid increases it will push the lid down, so the straw will pivot on the side of the tin and the pin will swivel up. If the air pressure on the lid decreases the pin will go down. When the air is heavy and presses down, the pressure is said to be high. If the air is light, the pressure is said to be low. High pressure often means that the weather will be dry. Low pressure often means that the weather will be stormy. Ask the class to compare their results against a real barometer.

Cross-curricular activities
- Read some books about adventures in the atmosphere: *Olaf's Incredible Machine* by Nicholas Brennan (Viking Kestrel), *Sun and Rain* by Ann Ruffell (Viking Kestrel/Puffin) and *Ossie Goes Supersonic* by Hunter Davies (Bodley Head/Armada).
- Demonstrate in Assembly how water is used in various religions for initiation ceremonies such as baptism, or as 'holy water'.
- Include in a history project the development by the Romans of aqueducts to carry water over long distances.

Summary
- A layer of air called the atmosphere surrounds the Earth.
- Air is all around us. It has weight and its pressure is the same from all directions.
- Close to the Earth the air is very thick, but further up in the atmosphere it thins out.
- Moving air forms wind.

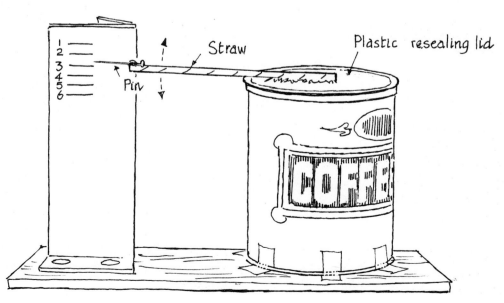

The children should be introduced to a more detailed study of the composition of the solar system.

Level 4

Accustom the children to the passing of time by developing a project on their dates of birth, drawing graphs and charts.

Solar system

What you need

Nine balls, each a different colour, pencils, paper, cardboard, scissors, square pieces of transparent perspex sheeting, pieces of light wood to make a frame, handles and screws, tracing paper, white cardboard.

What to do

In order to give the children an idea of the scale of the solar system and the relative distances of the planets from the Sun, make a model of the system in the playground or school hall. Write the name of a planet on each of the differently coloured balls. Use a larger ball to represent the Sun. Place this ball in the centre of the space available. Then get the children to measure the following distances from the Sun and place each 'planet' in order, to gain some idea of the proportions of the solar system:

Mercury: 39 cm. Venus: 72 cm. Earth 1m. Mars: 1.5m. Jupiter: 5.2m. Saturn: 9.5m. Uranus: 19.2m. Neptune: 30m. Pluto: 39.4m.

● Give the children an idea of the relative sizes of all the planets by letting them make scale models out of cardboard, cutting each model into a circle of the diameter suggested below. (If there is not enough space, divide each measurement by two.)

Mercury: 3.8cm. Venus: 9.6cm. Earth: 10cm. Mars: 5cm. Jupiter: 109.5cm. Saturn: 90.2cm. Uranus: 37.2cm. Neptune: 37.2cm. Pluto: 4.8cm.

● Let the children make a map of the stars in the sky. Give each child a frame of wood around a square sheet of transparent perspex.

Screw a handle to the bottom of each frame. Help the children to use a star-chart to find the star called Polaris. Ask each child to mark the position of Polaris on the frame.

Polaris is called the North Star because it is always in the same position in the sky. When the children have fixed Polaris on their charts, let them take them home and use them in their gardens at night. Ask them to try to find some more well-known stars, with the help of their parents and using star-charts, and enter these on their perspex charts. When they come back to school they could trace the stars from the perspex on to tracing paper, and then transfer them on to white cardboard and write the names of the stars underneath. All the charts could be put into a class 'Atlas of the Heavens'.

Level 5

Phases of the Moon
What you need
Pencils, paper.

What to do
Encourage the children to study the phases of the Moon over a period of one month, and relate these phases to the shapes shown below, drawing pictures and maps.

Information technology
Take the children to a planetarium to observe a model of the solar system.

Cross-curricular activities
● Stories about the Earth in space include *Of Time and Stars* by Arthur C Clarke (Gollancz), *Moonwind* by Louise Lawrence (Collins), and *Space Hostages* by Nicholas Fisk (Puffin).
● Link a study of Earth in space with the early maritime explorations of navigators like Magellan and Columbus, and their use of globes and navigating equipment.
● Make a study of practical map-reading – introduce the children to contours, grids and symbols, using Ordnance Survey maps.

Summary
● The solar system derives its name from the Latin *sol*, or sun.
● The Sun is a huge star in the centre of the solar system.
● Nine planets move around the Sun. These are Mercury, Venus, Earth, Mars, Jupiter, Saturn, Uranus, Neptune and Pluto.
● The movement of the Earth provides us with night and day and the seasons.
● The light of the Moon comes from the Sun, and is reflected off the Moon's surface.
● The Moon appears to change shape because different parts of it are illuminated by the Sun as the Moon changes position during its regular progress around the Earth.

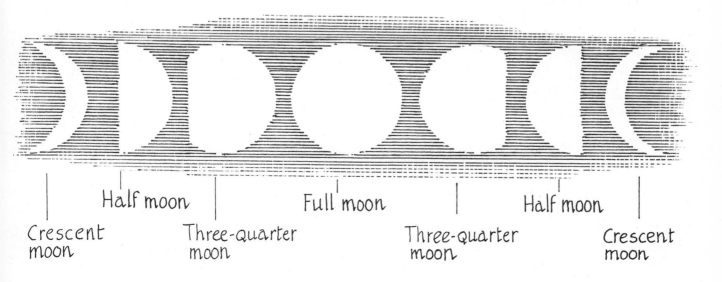

Crescent moon — Half moon — Three-quarter moon — Full moon — Three-quarter moon — Half moon — Crescent moon

Encourage the children to study their surroundings and to differentiate between natural and man-made materials. They should have a chance to study the similarities and differences between materials.

Level 3

Comparing bridges
What you need
Pictures of bridges from books, magazines or newspapers, pencils, paper, equipment for model-making such as pipe cleaners, card, adhesive, lengths of wood.

What to do
Make a study of bridges in the area, or collect pictures of different types of bridges. What are they made of? How are they constructed? What do they cross? Let the children look for natural bridges such as logs. Manufactured bridges include beam bridges, stretching across a river or road, perhaps supported by pillars, suspension bridges, hanging from steel wires or towers and arched bridges, supported by arches of masonry. Ask the children to consider the strengths and weaknesses of each type. What condition are the bridges in? Are they as important and useful now as when they were first built? Let the children sketch the bridges and make models of them using various different materials.

Natural versus manufactured materials
What you need
Small stones, clay, empty matchboxes, sand, cement, water, marbles, scraps of wood, elastic bands.

What to do
In a study of natural and manufactured materials, let the children make two model

Beam

Arch

Suspension

walls and test them for strength. First they should make a natural wall out of small stones, fitting them carefully together. Then they could make a manufactured wall out of home-made model bricks made by putting some clay in matchbox trays and baking the bricks in the sun. When the bricks are dry, the children should tip them out and make mortar by mixing three parts sand to one part cement, with just enough water to bind the sand and cement together. They can stick the bricks together to form a small wall, using the mortar.

Ask the children to compare the two walls. Which seems the stronger and more useful? Encourage the children to devise some tests of the walls' strength, for example by rolling a marble down a ramp or carefully firing a piece of wood from a catapult at them. When might the natural stone wall be more useful than the brick one?

● Conduct a number of investigations in which manufactured items are compared with natural ones. Compare the efficacy of a whisk with the stirring capabilities of a piece of wood, and so on. Why have people always tried to improve upon natural materials?

Varieties of rock

What you need
Glass container, small shell, leaves, sand, gravel, humus, plaster of Paris, water, pin, empty carton.

What to do
Introduce the children to different kinds of rock. Sedimentary rock is formed over a long period, under immense pressure from the earth and water above it.

Let the children make a sedimentary rock. In a glass container they should place a small shell, some leaves, a tablespoonful each of sand, gravel, plaster of Paris and humus. They should mix these into a paste with some water, pour the paste into an empty milk carton and leave it for several hours. Next, let the children make some small holes in the bottom of the carton with a pin, and place the carton in a sink for a few days to drain. Then they can cut the carton away and examine the mixture. The part which has fallen to the bottom should be turning into a form of sedimentary rock.

Testing the strength of materials

What you need
Thin cardboard, gummed paper, tin, sand, assortment of threads — cotton, yarn, wool — empty yoghurt pot, thin wire, marbles.

What to do
Let the children test the strength of some paper pillars. Ask them to make a number of pillars of different sizes and shapes out of thin cardboard and gummed paper. Stand the pillars upright. Place a piece of cardboard across the top of each pillar and put a tin on top of the cardboard. The children should pour sand into the tin until the pillar sags or collapses under the weight, and then weigh the amount of sand in the tin. Compare the amounts of sand needed to make each pillar collapse. Is there any correlation between the size or shape of the pillar and the amount of sand it can support?

● Ask the children to test the strength of various different types of thread. The pieces of thread should all be the same length. The children should suspend the threads from a beam or support, and suspend an empty yoghurt pot, with a piece of wire as a handle, from the end of each length of thread in turn. Place marbles in the pot one at a time until the thread breaks under the strain. Note the number of marbles it takes to break each piece of thread. Which is the strongest thread, and which is the weakest? How could the children use this knowledge when manufacturing something?

Level 4

Comparing the porosity of bricks
What you need
Assortment of bricks, buckets of water.

What to do
The children could begin comparing the simple properties of materials by investigating how bricks stand up to weather conditions. Find a number of different bricks, and let the children examine them. In which ways are the bricks similar? Ask the children to weigh each brick, and then place each in a bucket of water for four hours. Then they should weigh the bricks again. Are they heavier than they were before? If so, what does this mean? Which type of brick would the children use to build a house? Would they prefer a brick which soaks up a lot of water or one which does not?

Comparing the strengths of bridges
What you need
Cardboard, books, coins.

What to do
Comparisons of this nature can be applied to everyday materials; for example by comparing the strengths of different kinds of bridges. Let the children make a model of an ordinary beam bridge by placing a length of cardboard across two piles of books. They should then place coins on top of one another in the middle of the bridge until the bridge collapses.

Then they can take another piece of cardboard, the same size and shape as the first, and turn it into an arched bridge by bending it and supporting the base of each side against the books. Ask the children to place coins on top of the centre of the arched bridge. Which bridge supported more coins before sagging or breaking? What can be deduced from this? Could either bridge be strengthened in order for it to support more coins?

Weighing solids and liquids

What you need
Assortment of containers, variety of liquids.

What to do
It is important that the children grasp the principle that solids and liquids have 'weight' and occupy volume. Find containers of different shapes, including saucers, dishes and moulds. Fill each one with water.

What do the children notice about the shape that the water takes in each container? What does this mean? Repeat the experiment with several different liquids. Does the same thing happen?

Collect a number of different materials — metal, rock and wood — all roughly the same size. Ask the children to investigate the materials. Do they all weigh the same? Do they all occupy roughly the same amount of space? Do they all displace the same amount of water?

Heating solids

What you need
Block of ice, frying pan.

What to do
Demonstrate but do not allow the children to participate in an experiment to determine what happens when a block of ice is heated in a frying pan. Let them watch the ice. What does it change to first? What does it change to next? What has happened? (The ice changes from solid to liquid to gas.)

Solids, liquids and gases

What you need
Pencils, paper, liquids, solids.

What to do
Classify materials into solids, liquids and gases according to their properties. Ask the children to make a list of five solids and five liquids, and to collect examples of them. They should also try to collect a number of gases, including perhaps steam, and carbon dioxide made by breathing out on a cold day.

Level 5

Weighing gases

What you need
Water, jar, kettle.

What to do
Gases also have weight. Ask the children to measure some water in a jar and pour the water into a kettle. Let the kettle boil for a few minutes, allow the water to cool, and then measure it again. The water remaining will weigh less because some of it has been turned into steam.

Classifying rocks

What you need
Vinegar, eye-dropper, stones and pebbles, gummed labels, pencils.

What to do
Testing and classifying may be carried out in many ways. It is possible to test rocks to see if they are limestone or chalk, two of the commonest kinds of sedimentary rock. Take some vinegar and put it in an eye-dropper. Place a drop of vinegar on a variety of stones and pebbles. If bubbles appear on the surface where the vinegar has been applied, then it is a sedimentary rock. The chemicals in the vinegar have this effect on limestone and chalk. Ask the children to label the rocks which have been shown to be sedimentary.

Separating mixtures

What you need
Sand, salt, water, containers, filter paper, funnel, sea water, saucer.

What to do
As well as mixing things together, the children should be given practice in separating mixtures. They could start by trying to separate a mixture of sand and salt. Salt will dissolve in water, while sand will not, so the two can be separated in the following way.

Make an equal mixture of sand and salt. Stir the mixture together, and add some hot water to it. This should dissolve the salt. Put a filter paper inside a funnel folding it so that it fits neatly. Place a container under the funnel, and pour the sand, salt and water mixture into the funnel. The water should drip through the filter paper into the container below, taking the salt with it. The sand will collect on the filter paper in the funnel.

Allow the water in the container to evaporate. Is the salt left in the container? Has the salt been separated from the sand? Ask the children to describe what has been done.

● If possible, collect some sea water. Place it in a saucer to dry in the sun. When the water has evaporated, what is left?

Information technology

Use television programmes and videos to show different types of gases and how they are formed.

Cross-curricular activities

● Introduce the children to books which show materials being used or changed in an interesting manner. Some stories which deal with substances which change are *Charlie and the Great Glass Elevator* by Roald Dahl (Puffin) and *Trillions* by Nicholas Fisk (Hamish Hamilton/Puffin).
● Use work on walls and bridges as part of a project on building by the Romans.
● Study the history of building, from the homes of the first people in caves, through the development of stone huts, wattle and daub huts, and so on to the present day.
● Make a natural product — clay — into a manufactured one — pottery. Create a simple bowl by squeezing clay into shape. Leave it to dry for a day, and then bake or fire it. Cover it with the powdered glass known as glaze, and then bake or fire the pot again.

Summary

● All objects on earth are made up of millions of tiny molecules.
● The molecules in a solid are very close together. A solid is usually hard and has a shape of its own.
● In a liquid, the molecules are further apart than they are in a solid. A liquid is 'runny'. It spreads to cover a surface and takes the shape of any container it is put in.
● The molecules in a gas are even further apart than those in a liquid. A gas is light and has no shape of its own. It can go anywhere and fill any shape it is given.
● Under certain circumstances, substances may change their consistency.
● If molecules in a substance change their order, the substance will change from solid to liquid to gas, or vice versa.

At this stage the children should be introduced to a study of chemical reactions, the uses and properties of materials and change in materials.

Level 4

Chemical reactions
What you need
Two large nails, paint, jar of water, wire wool, container with lid, salt, indigestion tablet, health salts.

What to do
The children should be encouraged to study change in the environment around them — day into night, the seasons, the growth of plants and so on.
● Let them observe chemical change through an examination of the way in which rust is formed. This change is brought about by metal combining with oxygen in the presence of moisture. Obtain two large nails, and cover one of them with paint. Put both nails in a jar of water. After a week, examine them both. Is there a difference between them? Can the children understand what has happened?
● Next, put some wire wool in a sealed container. Place some more wire wool in a container of salt and water. Leave this container in the open so that air can get at it as well. After several days, examine both sets of wire wool. Can the children see a difference between them? What might have caused this?
● Change is an important part of chemistry. Place an indigestion tablet containing sodium bicarbonate in a glass of water. The tablet will then operate as though it had been swallowed. What happens to the tablet? What has caused this?
● Place a spoonful of health salts in a glass of water. Stir the water. The salts should be working in the water. What has happened to the salts? What has happened to the water? What changes have taken place?

● As an example of physical change, watch ice-cubes melt into water and then boil into steam. What has happened on each occasion?

Useful products from raw materials
What you need
Lemon, paint brush, container, piece of paper, access to an oven.

What to do
Raw materials may be converted into useful products by chemical change. Ask the children to squeeze the juice of a lemon into a glass or container, and then dip a paint brush into the lemon juice. They can then write a message on a piece of paper, dipping the brush frequently in the juice. They should leave the juice on the paper to dry; it will disappear. To make the message appear again, put the paper in a very low oven for about a quarter of an hour. What chemical change has taken place?

Level 5

Raw materials in manufacture

What you need
Clay, sand, strips of plywood, craft knife, adhesive, strong thread, tissue paper, twine, long cork, knitting needle, strips of plastic.

What to do
In order to demonstrate that air, water, rocks, wood and fossil fuels are all sources of raw materials for use in manufacture, encourage the children to plan and make a number of objects out of raw materials.
● Make bricks by mixing clay with a little sand. Shape each brick and put them to dry in an oven, on a radiator or in the sun.
● Make a kite from some very light wood shaped into a cross, with one strut longer than the other. Join the struts by cutting a notch half-way along the shorter strut, and another close to the top of the longer strut. Stick the struts together at the notches. Use a strong thread to bind the struts. Cover the kite with tissue paper, using adhesive to fix it in place. The finished kite should be diamond-shaped. Fix a long length of twine to the bottom and fly the kite in a good wind.
● Water can be used to power a model water-wheel. Collect a long cork, a knitting needle and eight strips of plastic cut to the same length.

Stick the knitting needle through the length of the cork, so that it pokes out on either side. Cut eight radial slots, equally spaced, down the sides of the cork. Stick the strips of plastic into the slots so that they stick out from the cork like the slats of a water-wheel.

Hold the water wheel under the running tap in a sink. What happens? Can the children think what a full-sized water-wheel could be used for?

Biochemical processes

What you need
Drinking glasses or containers, sugar lumps, assortment of powders such as flour and soap-flakes, water, pencils, paper.

What to do
In order to help the children to understand the application of biochemical processes, conduct experiments involving dissolving and assimilation.

Let the children pour a glass of water and taste it. Then they should drop a lump of sugar into the glass. After an hour has passed, let them taste the water again. Does it seem different now? Can they say in what way is it different? What do they think has happened to the sugar? What has happened to the water? What changes have taken place?

Collect a number of different powders. Ask the children to put each powder in a different glass of clean water. Ask them to observe and write down what happens to the powder each time. They should put each powder in one of three lists; 'Dissolved', 'Partially dissolved', and 'Not dissolved'.

Information technology
Make a practical study and comparision of washing machines and the way they clean clothes. Which seem the most effective? How can you judge this?

Cross-curricular activities
As part of a project on change make a study of the changing clouds in the sky, taking photographs and making drawings. Try to identify the main cloud formations – cirrus, high with dense heads; cirrocumulus, very high, piled up; cirrostratus, very high, shapeless; altostratus, medium high; altocumulus, medium high, piled up; stratus, low, shapeless; and cumulo nimbus, towering thunder clouds.

Summary
● Change is an important feature of chemistry.
● Different substances may react to one another when they are put together.
● A physical change occurs when the appearance of something alters.
● A chemical change occurs when a new substance is made through the action of one substance on another.

This target is concerned with the constitution of matter; it deals with atoms, and changes in the structure and properties of materials.

Level 4

Introduce the idea of atoms by considering the concept of smallness. Ask the children to make an extensive collection of small items. See how many objects smaller than a 1p piece they can assemble.

Changes of state and solubility

What you need
Candle, matches, matchbox, saucers, vinegar, sugar, drinking glasses, stop-watch.

What to do
Conduct investigations into changes in properties. Heat some candle wax until it melts. Ask the children which state the wax was in before it melted. What does it turn into when it is melted? Leave the melted wax in a saucer. What happens? What do the children think causes these different stages?

● Ask the children to pour some vinegar into a saucer, and then stand back a few steps. Using a stop-watch, they should work out how long it is before they can smell the vinegar. In which direction does the smell seem to be travelling? Some of the vinegar has evaporated and drifted into the air. Part of the vinegar has changed from a liquid – do the children know what it has changed to?

● Perform an experiment to show a chemical reaction. Strike a match on the side of a matchbox. What happens? There has been a reaction or change. By scraping one thing — the head of the match — against another — the side of the box — a third state has come about. What is this third state?

● Put a lump of sugar in a glass of cold water. Place another lump of sugar in a glass of hot water. Observe what happens to both lumps. Do they both end up in the same state? Is there a difference in the time it takes each lump to change its state? What is the reason for this difference?

Level 5

Molecules and atoms
What you need
Piece of charcoal, goggles, paper towels, hammer, marbles, ice tray, water.

What to do
It is not easy to give the children an understanding of molecules and atoms, but it is possible. Place a piece of charcoal on a paper towel. Wearing goggles, beat the charcoal with a hammer until it is ground into the finest dust possible.

Explain that the smallest, finest piece of charcoal is much bigger than any molecule. There will be many molecules in every particle of dust. In turn, there will be many atoms in each molecule.

Demonstrate how molecules might look if we could see them by placing some marbles in a tray of water. Put the tray in the freezer compartment of a refrigerator until the water has frozen.

Tell the children to imagine that the marbles are molecules. This resembles the way they would look inside a solid. Wait until the ice has melted, and ask the children to look at the marbles again. This is how molecules would look inside a liquid. Remind the children that there are many atoms in each molecule.

Information technology
Let the children use a variety of magnifying glasses and microscopes to develop the idea that the tiniest objects may be enlarged for the purpose of examination.

Cross-curricular activities
● Books which help develop in children an idea of change and smallness include *Sylvester and the Magic Pebble* by William Steig (Collins), a good adaptation for children of *Gulliver's Travels* by Jonathan Swift, and *The Shrinking of Treehorn* by Florence Parry Heide (Puffin).
● Introduce the children to a study of nuclear energy in a project on power.

Summary
● An atom is the smallest part of an element that can exist and still keep the properties of that element.
● Atoms are not usually found on their own, but exist in molecules.
● A molecule is a group of atoms and is also very small.

This section deals with movement and stopping, floating and sinking, forces and structures, forces and shapes, and gravity.

Level 3

Experiment with movements. How many ways of moving can the children demonstrate? Is it easier to move on the flat or on a slope? What do the children have to do when they run up a hill? How long does it take to slow down and stop on different surfaces?

Effects of forces on objects
What you need
Four pieces of wood, sand, square piece of paper, pins or tacks, toy vehicles, short plank, elastic band, books.

What to do
Demonstrate to the children that when things are changed in shape, begin to move or stop moving, forces are acting upon them.

Start by arranging four pieces of wood in a square to support a piece of paper. Pin the paper across the wooden frame. Start pouring sand on to the paper. The paper should go through a number of changes of shape, sagging, tearing and breaking under the force of the sand. Ask the children to record and discuss these changes.

● The children could then look at the degree of force needed to pull toy vehicles up a ramp. First they should make a ramp by resting a short plank against two books. Next, ask them to fix a rubber band to the front of a toy vehicle, and pull the vehicle up the ramp by the rubber band. Ask them to measure how much the band stretches from its normal position. Let them add two more books to the ramp, increasing the degree of slope, and pull the toy up this steeper ramp. They should measure how much the band stretches this time. They can repeat the experiment with two additional books on the pile, and compare the measurements. When was the band stretched furthest? What would cause this? What does it mean? Ask the children to estimate the degree of stretch they would expect to see in the band if there was only one book supporting the ramp.

● Make a ramp with four books and a short plank. Roll a toy vehicle from the top of the plank. Measure the distance it covers from the foot of the plank across a flat surface before it stops. Repeat this experiment, supporting the plank by three books, two books and then one book. Finally, place the vehicle on a flat surface and observe what happens. When did the truck travel the furthest? Why? Why did it not move when placed on a level surface?

Floating and sinking
What you need
Empty medicine bottle with screw top, basin of water, piece of string, heavy object for a weight, sand.

What to do
When the children start to think about the factors which cause objects to float or sink in water, they should realise that an object floats because it displaces its own weight in water. Float a medicine bottle with a screw top in a basin. The bottle will go down in the water a little way and push up the same amount of water as it has displaced. If we could weigh the water pushed aside it would weigh the same as the bottle of air.

● Show the children how the force of water pushes upwards on anything placed in it. Tie a piece of string around a heavy object and dangle it in the air. Let the children appreciate the weight of the object. Next, lower the object into a bucket of water. Ask the children to pull it up through the water by the string. Does it feel any different now? How? What causes this?

● The children could then progress to experimenting with how a heavy object can sink. Take the medicine bottle and remove the top. Float the bottle in a bowl of water. Pour some sand into the bottle. It should sink a little in the water. Remove the bottle, fill it with sand and screw the top on before replacing it in the water. This time it should sink. This is because the sand has pushed the air out of the bottle. The air weighed the same as the water it displaced. The sand weighs more than the water it pushes aside, thus making the bottle sink.

Level 4

Forces and movement
What you need
Flour, water, bowl, wooden spoon, hand whisk, electric beater.

What to do
The movement of an object depends on the size and direction of the forces exerted on it. Ask the children to stir some flour and water into a paste in a bowl, using a wooden spoon. How long does it take? Time the operation. Repeat the experiment with a hand whisk and then with an electric mixer, timing each operation. Which was the fastest method? Why was this?

Speed and road safety

What you need
Videos on road safety.

What to do
The local police force or road safety representatives could be involved in an experiment to show that the greater the speed of an object, the greater the force and/or time that is needed to stop it. Show that the faster anyone cycles the longer it takes him to stop, and the more force has to be applied to the brakes. Include this in a road-safety project. Get an adult to demonstrate the process, emphasising that it is dangerous. Do not allow the children to participate. Let the children watch videos on speed and the significance of this for road safety.

Gravity

What you need
Modelling clay, handkerchief.

What to do
An important force is the one which we call gravity, which attracts objects towards the centre of the Earth. Under most circumstances the size and weight of objects do not matter. They will reach the ground at the same time if dropped from the same height. Let the children drop some pieces of modelling clay of different weights and sizes from the same height. Do they hit the ground together?

The only time when this does not happen is when the force or resistance of the air catches certain objects and causes them to take longer to reach the ground. To illustrate this the children could drop three or four heavy objects to the group at the same time. At the same moment they could also release an open handkerchief. Does the handkerchief reach the ground at the same time as the other objects? If not, why not?

Measuring force

What you need
Clockwork railway engine, tracks, 50g weight, 100g weight.

What to do
Weight is a force and is measured in newtons. Place a clockwork railway engine on a circular track. Wind the engine up to its full extent and make a note of the number of times it goes round the track before stopping. Put a weight of 50g on the engine, and wind it to the full again. How many circuits does it make this time before stopping? Repeat the experiment with a weight of 100g on the engine. What is the difference in the number of circuits completed when increasingly heavy weights are put on the engine? What does this show?

Level 5

Investigating strengths of structures
What you need
Lollipop sticks, adhesive, bowl of water, small tins, sand.

What to do
There are a number of ways in which the children could investigate the strength of a structure. They could start by making a series of model rafts out of lollipop sticks stuck together with adhesive. Make them of different sizes and strengths, using different degrees of reinforcement. Float each raft in a bowl of water. Place a tin on each one, and pour sand on it until it sinks. Is there a connection between the strength of the raft and the force of the weight needed to sink it?

Friction on a moving object
What you need
Book, carpeted surface.

What to do
Ask the children to push a book along a piece of thick carpet. It will be difficult to move because of the friction caused by the two objects rubbing together. Ask the children to devise something which will go under the book and make it move more easily over the carpet.

Information technology
In a study of gravity, give the children the opportunity to use different electronic timing devices to assess the descent of objects dropped from heights.

Cross-curricular activities
● Introduce the children to stories involving forces of different sorts: *The Runner* by Cynthia Voigt (Collins), *Follow That Bus* by Pat Hutchins, (Bodley Head), *Speed Six* by Bruce Carter (Puffin) and *Flat Stanley* by Jeff Brown (Methuen/Mammoth).
● Link activities about floating and sinking to a study of the development of shipping over the ages. Encourage the children to find out how seafarers gradually developed bigger and safer craft for their voyages of exploration.

Summary
● The amount of force used to do something makes a difference to the speed with which it is done.
● A moving object will stop if an equal force acts against it from an opposite direction.
● Objects change shape if the forces acting upon them are strong enough.
● When an object is not moving relative to its environment, or when it is moving at a steady speed without a change of direction, there are balanced forces acting upon it.

The children should be shown how to construct and operate simple electrical circuits, work out which materials conduct electricity and which do not, and observe proper safety precautions.

Level 3

Ask the children to make a study of electricity as a source of lighting. How many different forms of electric light can they find? They could look at discos, sea-front illuminations, advertising signs and so on.

Levels 3 and 4

Making a circuit
What you need
Batteries, copper wires, bulbs, bulbholders.

What to do
The children should have practical experience, under supervision, of completing an electrical circuit and seeing it work. They could work in groups, each group assembling a battery, two wires and a small bulb in a holder.

First they should scratch off the rubber insulation at the ends of the wires, and unscrew the screw or terminal on one side of the top of the battery.

Next they should loop one end of the wire to the terminal and screw it back again, and then fix the other wire to the other battery terminal in the same manner.

Then they can take the two wires attached to the battery and wind the wires round the screws on the bulb holder, so there is one wire on each screw.

What happens? What happens if a wire is attached to only one of the holder screws? What does this tell us about the circuits or paths of electricity?

● The next activity should involve an investigation of the fact that some materials conduct electricity and others do not. Let the children repeat the first experiment with the circuit, but without removing the rubber insulation from either end of the wires. What happens? What happens when insulation is removed? What does this tell us about electricity and materials?

● Ask the children to write an account of the electrical circuits they have made and draw diagrams to explain what they have done.

Level 5

Varying the flow of electricity

What you need
Morse code transmitter, battery.

What to do
Show the children how to vary the flow of electricity in a simple circuit by attaching a Morse code transmitter to a battery. Tap out a simple SOS message in Morse.

Can the children see how these signals are obtained? What is happening to the flow of electricity in order to allow the message to be transmitted?

Information technology
Let the children use as many electric devices as possible, including perhaps computers and word processors.

Cross-curricular activities
● Introduce the children to stories involving the use of electricity as a source of power. You could include any children's version of *20,000 Leagues Under the Sea* by Jules Verne and *Tom's Amazing Machine Zaps Back* by Gordon Snell (Hutchinson).

● Make a study of the history of electricity from the early experiments of the Greeks with amber, which produced the term *elektron*, and Benjamin Franklin's experiments with flying a wet kite in a thunderstorm, to the perfection of the electric light bulb by Thomas Edison.

Summary
● Atoms contain a positively charged nucleus, around which negatively charged electrons orbit.

● Some electrons are tightly bound to the because of the attraction between these opposite charges.

● Some electrons are not as strongly attached and can easily be dislodged.

● If there is a nearby region of the material which has a positive charge, these electrons are attracted towards this region.

● The movement of electrons produces an electric current.

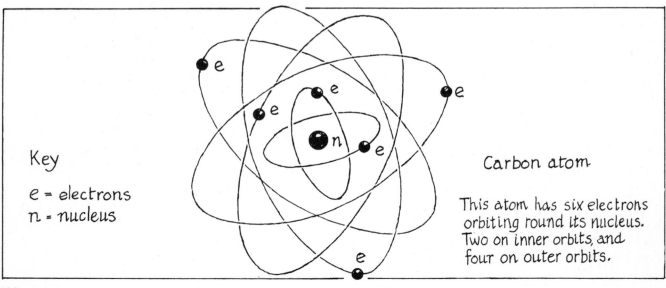

Key

e = electrons
n = nucleus

Carbon atom

This atom has six electrons orbiting round its nucleus. Two on inner orbits, and four on outer orbits.

The children should understand that machines and models need a source of energy in order to work, and that energy is essential to human life and activity.

Level 3

Encourage the children to find examples of machinery at work in the locality. How do the machines work? Which of them push? Which of them pull? Which of them turn? Do any of the machines use a combination of these movements?

Sources of energy
What you need
Balloons, adhesive, cardboard, polystyrene tray, yoghurt pot, assortment of toys powered by different sources, including water, wind, clockwork and electricity.

What to do
Experiment with various sources of energy. Ask the children to blow up a balloon, hold it by the nozzle, and then release it. What happens?

Control the flight of the balloon by blowing it up and placing a small cardboard ring inside the nozzle. What happens this time when the balloon is released?

● Continue to use air as a source of energy by constructing a model hovercraft. Assemble a polystyrene food tray, an empty yoghurt pot and some adhesive. Ask the children to place the pot with the open end downwards in the middle of the tray. Then they can draw a circle round the pot on the surface of the tray, and cut it out. Next, cut the bottom out of the pot, and fix the pot into the hole in the tray. Stick it into place. Then put the hovercraft on a flat surface and blow into it. What happens? What is the source of power?

● Develop this theme by asking the children to make a collection of toys powered by different sources – water, wind, clockwork and electricity. Let them examine each one and

describe its source of energy, using diagrams where possible. Which types of energy seem the most effective? Encourage the children to draw up a series of criteria by which the efficacy of the toys could be judged.

Temperature
What you need
Assortment of thermometers, bottles, water, ink, glass tubes, Plasticine, bucket.

What to do
The children should realise that temperature is a measure of heat and cold. They should use a variety of thermometers to note the range of temperatures in and out of the classroom.

They could try to make their own thermometers. Each group will need to fill a bottle with a mixture of water and a little ink. They should place a glass tube inside the bottle, with the top sticking out of the neck, and fix it in place with a piece of Plasticine at the neck of the bottle. The bottom of the tube should not touch the bottom of the bottle. Ask them to wait until the inky fluid settles a little way up the tube inside the bottle. On the outside of the bottle, they should mark lines up from the bottom. Next, the children should place the home-made thermometer in a bucket of warm water, making sure that the level of the water is not higher than the top of the thermometer. Does the level of the inky fluid rise? Ask them to note which line on the bottle it reaches.

Now let them place the thermometer in a bucket of very cold water. What mark does the inky water reach now? What does this mean?

Transferring energy
What you need
Toy bows and arrows with suction pads, gears.

What to do
To help children understand that energy can be transferred, allow them to experiment with power sources which transfer energy. Give the children some toy bows and arrows with suction pads, not points. Ask them to fit an arrow into each bow and pull back the string. The power is now stored in the bow-string. What happens to the power when the bow-string is released? Organize an archery contest for the class.

The children should also be given the opportunity to examine the use of gears in simple machines, for example a bicycle. What are the functions of these gears? How do they transfer energy?

Level 4

Food as energy
What you need
Variety of foodstuffs such as fruit, vegetables, bread, dairy products and chocolate, pencils, filter papers, paper.

What to do
Energy is essential to human life and activity as well as to models and machines. The fuel for this energy is provided by food. In particular, fats help to keep our bodies warm and provide us with energy.

Show the children a simple way to test different foods to see if they contain fat. Collect together some fruit, vegetables, bread, dairy products and chocolate. Draw each piece of food across a filter paper. If it leaves a greasy

mark it contains fat. Ask the children to make two lists; one of foods containing fat and the other of foods containing little or no fat.
● Encourage the children to devise ways of testing the amount of energy they use. After exercise, are they sweating? Are their hearts beating faster? Are they out of breath? Can they devise other tests to see if they have used extra energy?

Fuels as energy
What you need
Toy locomotives powered by steam, electricity and clockwork, tracks.

What to do
Just as food provides energy for people, so fuels are the energy suppliers for machines. Find three model locomotives, one driven by steam, one by electricity and one by clockwork. Try out all three on the same track. Devise tests to find the most effective. What are the strong points of each type? What are the weak points?

Storing and transferring energy
What you need
Picture of tanks, matchsticks, elastic bands, cotton reels, candles, lollipop sticks.

What to do
Show that energy can be stored and transferred by making model tanks. Show the children pictures of real tanks first, and explain the functions of these vehicles. Then each child can be given the materials to manufacture a simple tank. Using a matchstick to keep it in place, they should fix an elastic band at one end of a cotton reel. Ask them to thread the band through the hole in the middle of the reel. Then they can take a slice of a candle with a hole in the middle, thread the band through the hole in the candle and loop it over a lollipop stick. Twist the elastic band tightly round, and set the tank in motion. What form of energy is being used? How was it stored? How was it transferred?

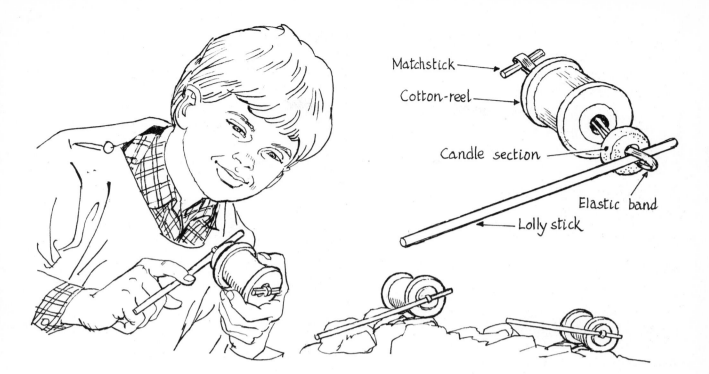

Matchstick

Cotton-reel

Candle section

Elastic band

Lolly stick

Level 5

Fuel economy and efficiency

What you need
Assortment of tins with lids, hot water, cotton wool, velvet cloth, pieces of paper, thermometer.

What to do
Ask the children to investigate the efficiency of different forms of insulation. Fill a number of tins with hot water at the same temperature. Make sure that the water is not too hot and that there is a secure lid on each tin. Leave one tin as a control, but ask the children to wrap different coverings round each of the others – cotton wool, velvet, paper and so on. After a few hours, they can use a thermometer to check the heat of the water in all the tins. Which has retained the most heat? Which has retained the least heat? How could this information be used to save on the heating bills for a house or school?
● To emphasise the limited global resources around us, involve the children in a project on the world's dwindling supplies of timber. Ask them to think of ways of recycling paper – making papier mâché models, etc.

Information technology
Let the children use thermometers to assess energy and its effects.

Cross-curricular activities
● There are a number of children's books on the theme of energy and its uses, including *The Gremlin Buster* by Rosemary Hayes, (Viking Kestrel), *Dr Dolittle in the Moon* by Hugh Lofting (Cape), and *Robot Revolt* by Nicholas Fisk (Puffin).
● Link a study of energy with a project on the development of transport, particularly the growth of railways. Begin by looking at the early experiments with stationary steam engines, the work of Richard Trevithick and then the development of 'Puffing Billy' in 1813 by William Hedley, which led to the work of George Stephenson and the growth of the country's railway system.

Summary
● Energy provides the driving force for things and people.
● Food provides human beings and other animals with energy. Important for this are carbohydrates, which give bodies the energy to work, and fats, which help store energy and keep the body warm.

The children should participate in activities which demonstrate that sound travels, that it takes time to do so, that it travels through different materials and that the frequency of a vibrating source affects the pitch of the sound it produces.

Level 3

Involve the children in a variety of music-making activities, including singing, playing musical instruments and dancing.

Sound as vibration
What you need
Dried peas, drumskin, cymbal.

What to do
Provide the children with activities which show that sounds are produced by vibrating objects. Put some dried peas on top of a tightly stretched drumskin. Strike a big cymbal next to the drumskin. The peas will jump. The cymbal vibrated when it was struck, which caused the air to vibrate, and then the sound waves made the drumskin vibrate in turn.

Sound travels
What you need
Small cans, lengths of wire or string, tuning forks.

What to do
To help the children understand that sound travels through different materials, group them in pairs and ask them to make telephones from a long wire or piece of string attached to two cans. One child should talk into one of the cans while the other listens to the open end of the other can. The sound will only carry if the cord or wire is stretched tightly, allowing the vibrations to travel.

The children could also experiment with the sounds made by tuning forks. Sound travels more easily through metal than through air.

Level 4

Sound and speed
What you need
Starter's pistol.

What to do
In the following activity, the children can observe for themselves that it takes time for sound to travel. Station the children a safe distance away, and fire a starter's pistol into the air. Ask the children what they notice about the time when the smoke appears as the pistol is fired and the time when they hear the report of the shot. What does this mean?

● The children can also use this experiment to discover how far sound can travel. One child should put his ear to the ground while a second child taps on the ground nearby. Can the sound be heard? They should repeat the experiment at varying distances. How far does the second child have to go before the first child can no longer hear the tapping?

Level 5

Pitch

What you need
Elastic band, guitar, three tins — one large, one medium-sized and one small — pencils, ruler, water, bottle.

What to do
The children should enjoy these experiments to discover that the frequency of a vibrating source affects the pitch of the sound it produces. They could start by altering the pitch of an elastic band stretched between the two fingers of one hand. They should pluck the band with one finger, and then tighten the band and pluck it again. Let them repeat the experiment, on each occasion pulling the band out further. Ask them to observe the frequency of the vibrations each time the band is extended further, and note the difference in pitch each time. Do the number of vibrations alter the pitch?

● Pluck one string of the guitar. Ask the children to watch the string. What does it do? What can they hear? Tighten the string and pluck it again. What does the string do this time? Does the pitch of the guitar change when the string is made tauter?

● Ask the children to place one small, one medium-sized and one large tin side by side upside down, and hit each tin several times with a pencil. Is there a difference in the pitch of the sound produced by each tin? Is there a connection between the size of the tin and the pitch?

● Place a ruler over the edge of a desk, so that half the ruler is on the desk and half jutting out. Hold the end of the ruler on the desk, and pluck the end which is sticking out. Ask the children to listen to the sound. Move the ruler out further, so that three-quarters of it is jutting out. Again, pluck the edge and ask the children to listen to the sound. Keep adjusting the ruler and plucking the end. Is there a difference in the pitch of the sound each time? Is there a connection between the pitch and the amount of the ruler jutting out over the desk? Does this have anything to do with the amount of the vibrations?

● Let the children pour water into an empty bottle. Does the pitch of the sound made by the water alter as the level of water rises in the bottle? They could repeat this experiment with bottles of different sizes.

Vibrations and loudness

What you need
Drums, or empty tins covered with rubber or plastic sheeting, corks.

What to do
Compare vibrations and loudness. First obtain some drums, or make them by stretching rubber or plastic sheeting over the mouths of a number of tins. Put a cork on the top of each drum. Let the children hit the drums softly. How much does the cork jump or vibrate? When they hit the drums harder, is the sound louder in each case? Does each cork vibrate more? What does this mean?
● Emphasise the importance of noise control by conducting a class investigation into quiet and noisy places near the school. Are there ways in which noisier places could be made quieter?

Information technology
Let the children use a tape-recorder to record noise in the environment.

Cross-curricular activities
● Introduce the children to stories about sounds or music: *The Trouble with Donovan Croft* by Bernard Ashley (Puffin), *Mr Majeika and the Music Teacher* by Humphrey Carpenter (Viking Kestrel), and *Mice and Mendelson* by Joan Aiken (Cape).
● Form a class orchestra consisting of home-made instruments. Let the children fill bottles with different amounts of water and blow across their tops, fill tins with dried peas and shake them, and so on.

Summary
● Sound travels when vibrations disturb the molecules of the air; this disturbance eventually reaches the eardrums, which also vibrate. Messages pass from the eardrums to the brain, which interprets the sound.
● The loudness of the sound is increased by the strength or energy with which an object vibrates.
● There are high and loud sounds; the level of sound is called the pitch.

At this stage the children should be helped to understand that light travels fast and in a straight line, but can be made to change direction, that light can be reflected, and that we see objects because light is scattered off their surfaces into our eyes.

Level 3

Silhouettes
What you need
Large pieces of white paper, torch, pencils.

What to do
Make a study of shadows. Stick a large piece of white paper on the wall and ask a child to sit sideways in front of the paper. Draw the blinds and turn out the lights. Ask another child to shine a torch on the head of the child in the chair. His head should appear in silhouette on the white paper. Have a third child trace round this outline shadow with a pencil. Repeat this until every child in the class has an outline to colour in or paint.

Bending light
What you need
Spoons, pencils, glasses of water.

What to do
Show how light can be made to change direction, even though it travels in a straight line. It can be bent when it passes from air to water. Put a spoon in a glass of water. Ask the children to look at the place where the air and the surface of the water meet. Let them put in a second spoon, and observe this carefully from all angles. Finally they can put in a pencil, and observe this. In each case, the object should seem to bend where it joins the water. Air sends reflections to the eye quicker than water does. Water also sends light waves in a straight line, but in a different direction, which makes them appear to bend.

Mirrors

What you need
Paper, pencils, mirrors.

What to do
Start a study of mirrors by showing that whatever is reflected in a mirror is reversed. Ask the children to write messages, and then hold them up in front of mirrors. The handwriting will be back to front in the reflection. Ask the children to try to write short sentences that are back to front. Then they can hold them up to mirrors and read them.

Level 4

Reflection of light

What you need
Assortment of objects with polished surfaces.

What to do
We see reflections in a mirror because the surface is highly polished, causing the light rays to be reflected back in an orderly manner. Ask the children to see how effectively light rays are scattered back into our eyes from various objects — mirrors, the backs of spoons, shop windows, puddles, etc.

Light travels

What you need
Torches.

What to do
To show how quickly light travels, turn on the electric light in a darkened room. Ask the children how long it takes the whole room to light up, and what this means.
● The fact that light travels in a straight line can be shown by asking the children to shine torches in a darkened room. Do the beams of light travel in straight lines or are they curved?

Shadows

What you need
Chalk.

What to do
The children should understand that shadows are formed when something comes between the straight lines of the rays of light and the surface on which they would otherwise be shining. The size of a shadow varies according to the position of the light source.
● Let the children see how a shadow will grow and shrink in the course of a day.

Early in the day, ask one child to stand still while another chalks around her shadow. Every hour, ask the child to stand in the same spot and chalk around her shadow. At the end of the day, let the children examine all the shapes of the shadows. Do they differ in size? At which time of the day was the shadow child-sized? Where was the sun then? What does this mean?

Level 5

Light and colour
What you need
Prisms.

What to do
The concept that light can be reflected is not an easy one for children to grasp, but they could experiment with triangular prisms in order to see that while sunlight appears to be white it is really made up of a number of colours. Darken a room so that only one ray of sunlight shines in through a window. Place the prism of glass in the path of that ray of sunlight. Adjust the prism by turning it until a band of colours appears. These are the colours of the rainbow, or the spectrum: red, orange, yellow, green, blue, indigo and violet.

Information technology
Make a study of laser beams and their uses – for example at pop concerts.

Cross-curricular activities
● Introduce the children to stories involving light, colours and the sun: *Sun and Rain* by Ann Ruffell (Viking Kestrel) and *Green Smoke* by Rosemary Manning (Constable).
● Make a study of creatures, for example the tawny owl, that hunt by night instead of during the day.
● Let the children construct a toy camera.

First, they should cut the ends off a tin. Next, stick brown paper over one end and tissue-paper over the other. Make a pin hole in the centre of the brown paper. To use the camera, the children should put a cloth over their heads, look through the tissue-paper end of the camera and point the end with the brown paper towards the light.

As a design and technology exercise, ask the children to try to improve upon this basic toy camera.

Summary
● Light comes from the glowing gases of the Sun.
● We see things because light bounces off them and enters our eyes. This is called reflection.
● Light travels very quickly and consists of a number of different colours which blend and appear to be white.
● Each object on Earth will absorb most colours of the spectrum, but will bounce back or reflect predominantly one of the colours to our eyes.
● Only a small proportion of the light leaving the Sun ever reaches the Earth; much is reflected back into space from the clouds.
● The tiny amount of light which does reach the ground provides us with most of our light and energy.

Red
Orange
Yellow
Green
Blue
Indigo
Violet

Children should be given the opportunity to follow the course of a scientific advance, describing the life and times of the principal scientist involved. This can be linked with other curriculum subjects and can also be used for general revision purposes in the science curriculum. The topics suggested here are:
● Stone Age people and tools;
● Galileo and time;
● George Stephenson and the steam engine;
● Frank Whittle and jet propulsion.

Stone Age people and tools

The first men and women who wandered over the Earth more than two million years ago seem to have had no settled homes. They had no tools and could not make fire. They moved in small groups from place to place, living off roots, berries, grubs and the raw carcasses of the dead animals they found.

As thousands of years passed, they began to invent tools to help them. These first tools were rough and simple. Many of them may have been invented by accident. Someone might have discovered the use of a club when they found a large branch on the ground and used it to fight off a wild animal.

But sticks and branches were not strong enough for all purposes. They broke easily. The first strong tools were made out of stone. They were hard and strong and lasted a long time. Because of the use of stone, we call the period the Stone Age.

Collecting tools
What you need
Heavy, round stones, pointed stones, flat stones, classroom tools, paper, pencils.

What to do
Ask the children to imagine that they are Stone Age men and women. They should collect stones and rocks which they could use as tools. Make a class collection of round, heavy stones which could be used as hammers, pointed stones for use as saws or cutters, long, round stones which could be used as rollers and flat stones for use as scrapers.

Ask the children to devise tests for each of these tools. What would the Stone Age people have used them for? Ask them to assess the efficacy of each tool and write about it.

Make sure that the children can use all the tools in their classroom, including rulers, scissors, saws, chisels, planes and other equipment.

Creating tools
What you need
Paper, scissors, eggshell, Plasticine, adhesive, soap, glycerine, bowls of water, length of thin wire, pencils, long poles or broom handles, cotton reels, string, hooks, flints.

What to do
Ask the children to decide which tools they

will need to make a 'tough egg'. Ask each child to draw a circle on a piece of paper, cut out the circle and fold it in half. Then they should cut along the line to produce a semi-circle. Next they can roll the semi-circle into a cone in the shape of a witch's hat, and stick the edges together. Then ask them to take a clean eggshell and stick a piece of Plasticine about the size of a pea in the bottom. Stick the hat to the top of the egg. Paint a face on the egg. Put the egg on a desk and give it a push. What happens every time the 'tough egg' is pushed or flicked? Can the children make any improvements or alterations to this? What tools will they need?

● Ask the children to design and make their own simple tool for blowing bubbles. Make a bubble solution by putting some pieces of soap in a bowl of water and adding a mixture of water and a little glycerine to it. Can they fashion an implement for blowing bubbles, using a piece of thin wire?

● The first people may have moved heavy objects by putting them on rollers made of fallen tree trunks. Ask the children to move a heavy packet across a table, using six pencils as rollers. How will they accomplish this?

Can they repeat this activity on a larger scale, using six broom handles and something flat and heavy?

● When the Stone Age people wanted to lift something heavy, they might have done this by making a pulley; first throwing a creeper over a stout branch of a tree, then attaching the object to be lifted to one end of the vine and pulling on the other end.

The children can construct their own model pulleys with a cotton reel, some wire, a hook and some string. First they should fix the hook to the wall. Then they can pull the wire through the two holes of the cotton reel and join the wire together above the reel. Ask them to hang the cotton reel from the hook by the wire. Next they should put a piece of string over the cotton reel, and tie an object to one end of the string. They will be able to lift the object into the air by pulling the other end of the string. Can they see why the object is lifted so easily in this way?

● The Stone Age people found that flint was the best type of stone for making tools. It was

hard and strong, but could be chipped into shape. Let the children collect some different kinds of flint.

Further activities and discussion

Ask the children to make a study of the history of tools. What were tools made of when the Stone Age came to an end? How have they developed since then? Ask the children to use their discoveries to study the different types of tools available today. What are the most modern methods of hammering, cutting, rolling and scraping? What sorts of sophisticated pulleys are available today? Is flint used for anything today? Can they bring examples of modern flint products to school? Ask the class to discuss the importance of tools in agriculture through the ages.

Summary

● Tools need to be strong and durable.
● Stone was more effective than wood for the manufacture of tools, but even stone had its drawbacks. People were soon to look for even stronger materials.

Galileo and time

Galileo Galilei was a great scientist who made many important discoveries about the heavens and confirmed the theory of an earlier scientist called Copernicus that the Earth travelled round the Sun, not the Sun round the Earth as was generally thought.

Galileo was born in Florence in 1564. He was a brilliant university student, and was made a professor before he was 25. His first experiments were concerned with time, and with constructing the pendulum clock.

In 1609, Galileo heard that an instrument called a telescope had been invented in the Netherlands. Galileo made his own telescope which magnified things a thousand times. When he declared that the Earth moved round the Sun, the Church authorities were shocked because they maintained that the Earth was the centre of the universe. They forced Galileo to say that he no longer believed that the Earth travelled round the Sun. However, he continued his studies until his death in 1642.

Making a pendulum

What you need
Piece of cord or thick string, object for a weight, stop watch, sticks.

What to do
Ask the children to study and make some pendulums. Each child could make a pendulum by tying a weight to a stick by a cord. They should allow the weight to dangle from the stick, and then pull the pendulum to one side and use a stop watch to measure the time it takes for the pendulum to swing from one side to the other. Ask them to time the long swings, when the pendulum first starts to move, and then time the shorter swings, after the pendulum has been moving for some time. What do they notice about the time it takes each type of swing to complete its arc? Could this knowledge be used in the construction of a clock?

The children could then make two pendulums of the same weight but hanging from different lengths of cord. They should tie two cords on to one stick; one cord a metre long and the other half a metre long. Then they can suspend the weights from the cords, making sure that the cords are far enough apart on the horizontal stick for them both to swing freely.

The children should pull both pendulums back and let them start swinging at the same time. What do they notice about the swing of each pendulum? Do they both take the same time to complete an arc, or are the timings different? Could this information be used in the construction of a clock?

Let the children repeat the above experiment, this time using cords half a metre long and a quarter of a metre long. What do they notice this time about the time the pendulums take to complete an arc?

Making clocks
What you need
Stick, pegs, tin or plastic basins, hand drill, measuring jug, stop watch, bucket of water, stones, candles, matches, craft knife.

What to do
Let the children make an assortment of clocks of the type which were used before the pendulum clock was invented.

● Make a shadow clock by putting a stick in the ground on a sunny day. With a peg, mark the tip of the shadow cast every hour. Check the next day to see if the shadow falls on each peg exactly on the hour.

● A water clock is made by boring a hole in the bottom of a tin or plastic basin. Hang the tin or basin over a measuring jug and fill it with water. Watch the water drip through to the measuring jug. Using a watch, work out how long it takes for the water to rise to each measurement in the jug. Repeat the experiment several times to see if it takes the same amount of time in each case.

Another type of water clock may be made by filling a bucket with water and boring a hole in the bottom of a plastic bowl. Put several stones in the bowl and place it in the water. Using a watch, see how long it takes for the bowl to sink to the bottom of the bucket. Repeat the experiment to see if it takes the same time.

● A candle clock consists of two candles of the same size. Light one of them. On the unlit candle, make a mark at the place the lit candle has reached every fifteen minutes. The marked candle could then be lit and used to tell the time at 15-minute intervals.

Ask the children if they can devise any other kinds of clock. Test all the clocks and decide which are the most effective.

Making a telescope
What you need
Lenses, rulers, Plasticine.

What to do
See if the children can make a telescope, as Galileo did. Assemble for each child two lenses and a ruler. The children can use Plasticine to fix the two lenses some distance apart on top of the ruler. They should keep adjusting the lenses until they can see through them both at the same time. What can they see? What seems to happen? Is there anything unusual about what they can see through the telescope? What causes this?

Further activities and discussion
Encourage the children to discuss the concept of time, based on the experiments they have made. What is the importance of being able to measure the passing of time? What developments have been made in the design of clocks and watches over the last fifty years?

Summary
● People have made many attempts to devise machines which will record the passing of time. These include shadow clocks, water clocks, candle clocks, sun dials and hour glasses.

● The first weight-driven mechanical clocks may have been built in the ninth century.

● Galileo invented the pendulum when he discovered that it always takes the same time for the pendulum to swing from one side to the other and back again. Galileo's idea was taken up by people trying to design clocks.

George Stephenson and the steam engine

George Stephenson was born near Newcastle in 1781. He came from a family of six children, and his father had a job at a local coal mine.

The family was too poor to send the children to school. At the age of ten, George Stephenson was looking after cows for a farmer. He then became an odd-job boy in a coal-pit.

From an early age he showed great mechanical ability. He went to night school to learn to read and write and handle numbers. He became an engineer in several coal mines. Soon he had invented and built a range of stationary steam engines for pumping water out of pits. He then developed the work of Richard Trevithick and built an engine or locomotive strong enough to pull eight wagons along a track. When a railway line was built between Stockton and Darlington, George Stephenson was appointed the engineer for the line. In a Newcastle factory, he built his first great steam locomotive. It was a boiler on wheels, with a tall chimney. It was known as *Locomotion* and made its first journey in 1825. Later, he built an even greater steam locomotive known as the *Rocket*, which won a competition to see if a steam engine could pull a train along the newly-built railway track from Liverpool to Manchester.

Steam
What you need
Saucepan with lid, weights, water.

What to do
Help the children to study steam power, making sure that they do not come near the boiling water. Fill a saucepan with water and put a lid on it. Boil the water and ask the children to discuss what happens to the lid. How could this have given Richard Trevithick and George Stephenson the idea for steam-powered engines?

Repeat the experiment with a weight on top of the saucepan lid. Then put on a heavier weight and boil the saucepan again. What happens to the lid? What does this prove about the power of steam? Find out the heaviest weight which the steam will move when it forces itself against the lid of the saucepan. How could an engineer use this information to design an engine?

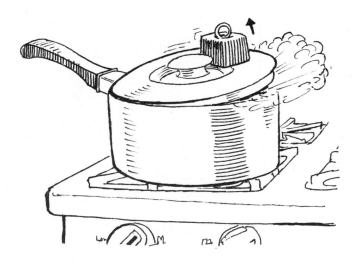

● Show that the steam which drives an engine is really water which has been changed by heat. With the children watching from a safe distance, direct a jet of steam from the spout of a kettle against a cold surface, such as the bottom of a saucepan. After a few moments the steam will change into something. What does it change into? What does this mean?

Conductors of heat
What you need
Jug of hot water, spoon, metal objects, piece of wood, pencils, paper.

What to do
Engineers often need materials which will allow heat to pass through them quickly. This means that when the material is placed next to something hot, it allows the heat to escape through it. As the children watch, put a jug of hot water on the table. Place a number of different objects in the water, with one end sticking out above the water. Use a spoon, a piece of wood, metal objects and a variety of other materials. Ask each child in turn carefully to touch the end of each object

protruding from the water. Some of the objects will be hot, others will not. The materials which get hot are said to be good conductors of heat. Make two lists and ask the children to place the objects they have touched in lists of 'Good conductors of heat' and 'Poor conductors of heat'.

Testing shapes
What you need
Sand, sand-tray.

What to do
When engineers are constructing their engines they have to ensure that their materials are the right shape for the functions they fulfil. Ask the children what would be the right shape for an implement to dig some sand from a sand-tray. Ask them to collect some different objects and test and adjust them until they have a suitable implement.

If the children wanted to sift some of the sand from a tray into a basin, what sort of a sieve could they devise? Ask them to make and test a number of sieves and decide on the most suitable.

Testing materials
What you need
Paint, transparent adhesive tape, microscope, assortment of surfaces approximately 10 cm x 10 cm.

What to do
Engineers also have to test materials to find out which are the most effective. Ask the children to find out which is the best surface for retaining paint. Ask the children to assemble some different materials with flat surfaces measuring about 10 cm by 10 cm. They could use different woods, metals, plastic, stone, plaster, cardboard, etc. Let the children apply an undercoat to each surface, wait until it is dry and then apply a top coat of paint. When the top coat has dried, ask the children to stick several large pieces of transparent adhesive tape to the surfaces and leave them for 24 hours. After this period, the children can rip the tapes off. Let them examine each tape under a microscope and look at each surface. Which surface has lost the most paint and

which has lost the least? Which surface seems the most effective for retaining a coat of paint?

Different kinds of power
What you need
Tube, bicycle pump, football adaptor, modelling clay, marble.

What to do
Explain to the children that other engineers in George Stephenson's era also experimented with different ways of powering engines. Tell the children the story of the inventor called Rammell who, in 1864, demonstrated what he called a 'tube train' at Crystal Palace. Rammell built a long enclosed tunnel and then, by applying pressure, propelled a coach through the tunnel and then sucked it back again.

Rammell's invention never caught on. Ask the children why they think it failed. Give them a chance to reproduce Rammell's invention in miniature. Each child will need a tube, a bicycle pump, a football adaptor and a marble. They should block one end of the tube with modelling clay and place the marble in the tube. Next they can insert the football adaptor through the modelling clay into the tube, having fixed it to the pump. Now they should pump hard. What happens to the marble? What would be the good and bad features of a railway system built on this principle?

Could the children, like Rammell, think of a way of sucking the marble back through the tube? Would a vacuum cleaner help?

Further activities and discussion
Ask the children to make a study of steam power. Ask them to discuss its advantages and disadvantages, based on the experiments they have undertaken. What is steam power used for today? Is it still used on most railway systems? If not, why not?

Summary
- A steam locomotive had a boiler full of water. This was heated by coal fires or, sometimes, by oil.
- The fire heated the water and turned it into steam.
- The force of the steam propelled the locomotive.

Frank Whittle and jet propulsion

Frank Whittle was a young RAF pilot who developed a method of powering aircraft by rockets. This was known as jet propulsion. When he was only 19, Whittle wrote an essay stating that aircraft of the future would be propelled by rockets. At first his ideas were rejected, but when war broke out in 1939 he was ordered by the RAF to design and produce jet fighters. In 1941 the jet-propelled aircraft had its first flight.

Rocket-propelled objects
What you need
Balloons, piece of thread, drinking straw, bulldog clip, adhesive tape, paper, scissors, pencils, plastic sheeting, aluminium foil tray, aluminium tube with top, adhesive, candles, matches, bowl of water.

What to do
Make a survey of rockets, using fireworks, and examine all aspects of their flight. Be very careful to maintain safety precautions.
- As a preliminary, ask the children to blow up four or five balloons. They should hold them by the nozzle and release them one at a time. In which directions do they go? Is there any pattern to their flight? If the children were trying to develop a rocket or flying machine, what would be the drawbacks of a flying object which behaved like the balloons just released? What sort of alterations would have to be made in order to improve the flying capability?
- Repeat the previous experiment, but this time get the children to control the flight of the balloon by providing it with guidelines. They should push a long piece of thread through a drinking straw and hang the thread across the classroom. Next, blow up a balloon and secure the nozzle with a small bulldog clip. Use adhesive tape to tape the balloon to the straw. Move the straw and the balloon to the end of the thread on one side of the classroom. Remove the bulldog clip. What happens? Ask the children to write about the guided flight of the balloon. What are its advantages? What are its drawbacks?

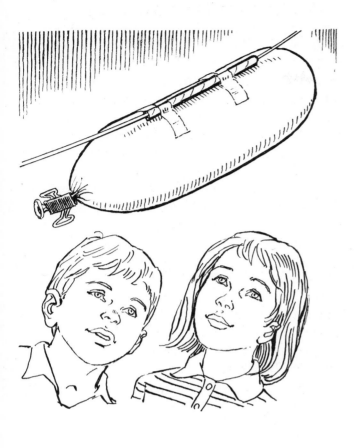

it is about 12 mm across, then tape it together. Make a second tube out of plastic film, which will not become wet when blown into. Adjust the size of this tube until it is 7½ mm in diameter. Blow up the balloon. Place the plastic tube inside the nozzle and the paper tube outside it, to keep the inner tube in place. Release the nozzle and let the balloon go. How does the flight of the balloon differ from the flights of the balloons with no tubes attached? Experiment with different-sized tubes inside and outside the nozzles of the balloons. Does the size of the tubes have any effect on the speed of the balloons? How do the nozzles affect the stability of the balloons?

● Ask the children to make more complicated rocket-propelled objects. They could make a model boat by taking an aluminium foil food-tray and an aluminium cigar tube. First they should glue the tube longways across the top of the foil tray, and half fill the tube with water. Before screwing the cap of the tube back on, they should bore a small hole in it. Next they can place three or four candle-ends on the tray beneath the tube, and place the tray in a bowl of water. Light the candles under the tube. The heat from the candles will turn the water in the tube into steam. This steam will shoot out of the small hole in the cap of the tube. (Remember to be very careful to stand back so that nobody can get scalded.) What does this escape of steam do to the tray? Ask the children to observe, discuss and write about what happens. Can they see what causes this?

● Try another way of controlling the flight of a balloon. Make two tubes, one to fit inside the nozzle of the balloon and the other to go outside it. Make the outer tube from drawing paper. Cut a strip 100 mm long and 70 mm wide. Cut off the corners and roll the strip round a pencil. Adjust the size of the strip until

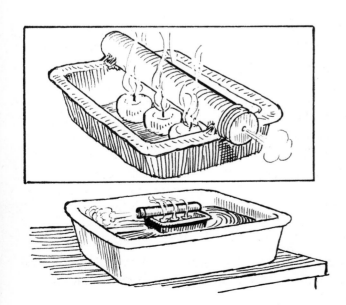

Pull of gravity

What you need

Tennis balls.

What to do

For hundreds of years before Frank Whittle's experiments, people tried to invent ways of flying through the air. They always fell back to earth because of the powerful pull of gravity, the unseen force which impels things to return to earth.

Ask the children to throw tennis balls into the air. How high can they throw the balls? No matter how high the balls go, what always happens to them?

Speed and pressure of air

What you need

Bicycles.

What to do

Scientists discovered that the faster an object moves through the air the greater is the force or pressure of the air upon it. Ask the children to carry out an activity to show this. Let them ride their bicycles on a level surface. Then ask them to ride their bicycles very carefully down a hill. Was the force of air in their faces when they went downhill different from the way it felt when they cycled on the level surface? If so, can they think of a possible reason for this?

Further activities and discussion

Ask the children to make a study of the history of flight, and to make and collect models of different kinds of aircraft, including paper and wooden gliders, and aircraft propelled by elastic or engines. Ask them to think about the reasons why Frank Whittle wanted to develop the use of rocket-powered flight. In what ways might it be more effective than other forms of flying? Ask the children to discuss this on the basis of the results of their observations and experiments.

Summary

A rocket produces hot gases which shoot out of the back of it, propelling it upwards or forwards in the direction in which it is pointed.

Chapter Five
Science-based projects

In this chapter, suggestions are given for incorporating the different attainment targets in projects.

The possibilities for topic work are numerous and teachers will come up with their own ideas for interesting projects. However, the topic webs outlined in this chapter may well provide a useful starting point. They have been grouped into four sets of projects: on living things; on materials; on the Earth; and on forces.

Projects on living things
AT1: Scientific investigation
AT2: Life and living processes

Projects on the Earth
AT1: Scientific investigation
AT3: Earth and environment

Projects on materials
AT1: Scientific investigation
AT4: Materials and their behaviour

Projects on forces
AT1: Scientific investigation
AT5: Energy and its effects

Projects on living things

The projects on living things suggested here are 'Trees', 'Life in water' and 'Change'.
● 'Trees' looks at the variety of trees and their needs, and considers the topics of seeds, the needs of trees for healthy growth, deforestation and the fossilisation of trees.
● 'Life in water' includes a study of ponds and pond life, the evolution of water creatures from prehistoric times, the habits of small water creatures, and shells.
● 'Change' looks at development in people, wildlife and plants, and involves work comparing different types of plants and different types of soil.

128

Projects on living things: Trees (AT2: Life and living processes)

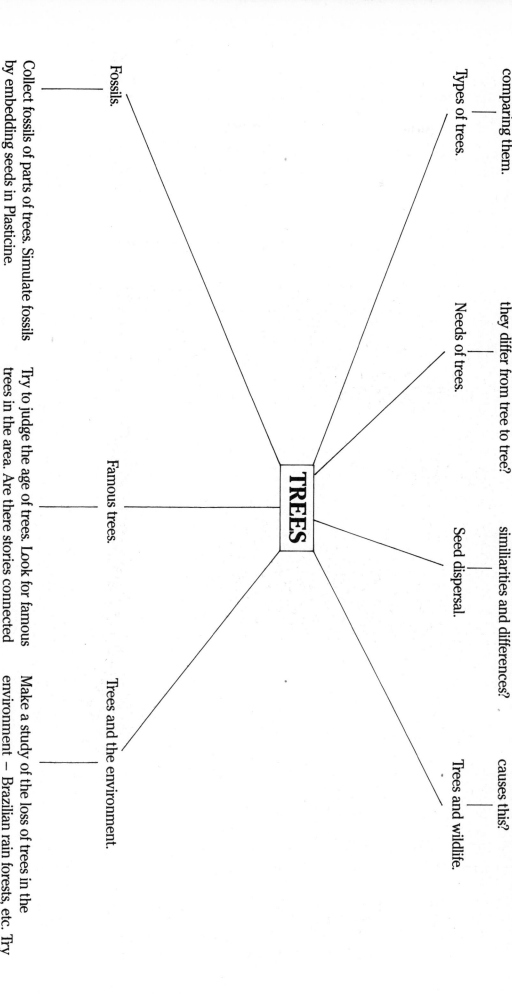

TREES

Types of trees.

Make a study of different trees in the area, drawing them, taking photographs, collecting leaves and comparing them.

Needs of trees.

Collect different parts of a tree – fruit, seeds, etc. What are the functions of each part? How do they differ from tree to tree?

Seed dispersal.

Make a collection of different seeds – acorns, etc. How are they dispersed? What are their similarities and differences?

Trees and wildlife.

How does wildlife growing and living in the shade of a tree differ from life further away? What causes this?

Trees and the environment.

Make a study of the loss of trees in the environment – Brazilian rain forests, etc. Try to become involved in an organized tree-planting project.

Trees and the environment.

Famous trees.

Try to judge the age of trees. Look for famous trees in the area. Are there stories connected to any trees? Are there any old wooden bridges or houses?

Fossils.

Collect fossils of parts of trees. Simulate fossils by embedding seeds in Plasticine.

129

Projects on living things: Life in water (AT2: Life and living processes)

LIFE IN WATER

Composition of a pond.

Study a pond and make a list of its component parts – mud, gravel, etc. Would it be possible, using a liner, to make a small pond somewhere on the school premises?

Pond life.

Make a collection of pond life in a glass container – insects, plants, etc.

Growth in ponds.

Make a study and collection of things beginning to grow in a pond – frogs' spawn, seeds, etc.

Development.

Follow the life cycle of a frog, from spawn to adult frog.

Small water creatures.

Use a microscope to study minute life in water. Use this as the basis for work on cells and their development.

Shells.

Make a collection of shells. Try to find out something about the original inhabitants of the shells.

Prehistoric creatures.

Make a study of the first creatures to live in water and creatures which left the water to make a life on land.

Project on living things: Change (AT2: Life and living processes)

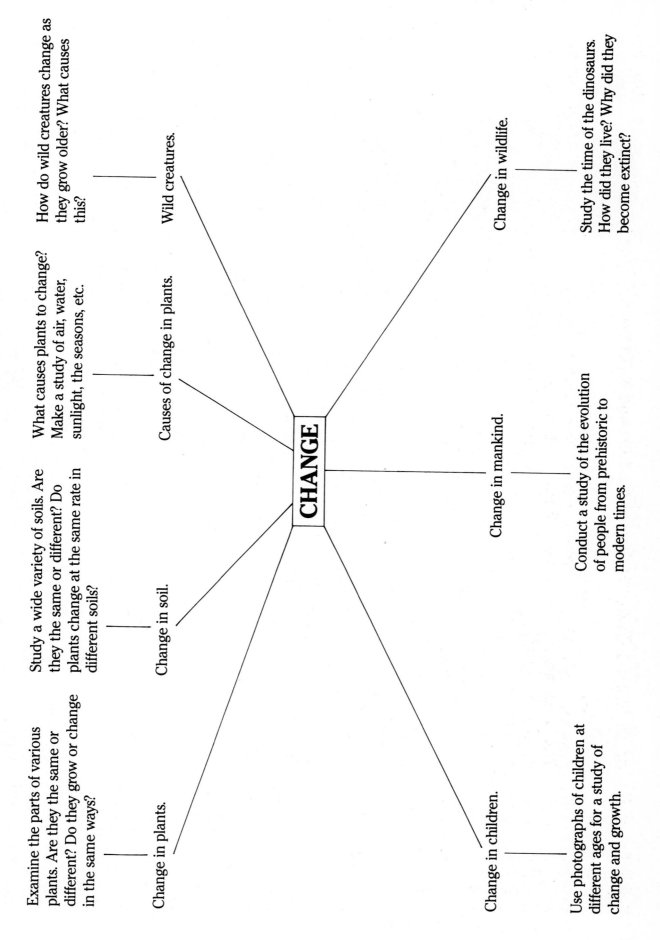

How do wild creatures change as they grow older? What causes this?

Wild creatures.

What causes plants to change? Make a study of air, water, sunlight, the seasons, etc.

Causes of change in plants.

Study a wide variety of soils. Are they the same or different? Do plants change at the same rate in different soils?

Change in soil.

Examine the parts of various plants. Are they the same or different? Do they grow or change in the same ways?

Change in plants.

CHANGE

Change in wildlife.

Study the time of the dinosaurs. How did they live? Why did they become extinct?

Change in mankind.

Conduct a study of the evolution of people from prehistoric to modern times.

Change in children.

Use photographs of children at different ages for a study of change and growth.

Projects on materials

The projects on materials suggested here are based around the topics of 'Clothes', 'Bridges' and 'Bricks'.

● 'Clothes' looks at how factors such as strength, warmth, safety and ease of cleaning affect our choice of materials when we are making or selecting clothes.

● 'Bridges' compares the different types of bridges which can be built, the characteristics of the main types, and the suitability of materials used in their construction.

● 'Bricks' discusses the properties of the different sorts of bricks which are available, and compares their characteristics. The project looks at the suitability of the different types for use in building.

Projects on materials: Clothes (AT4: Materials and their behaviour)

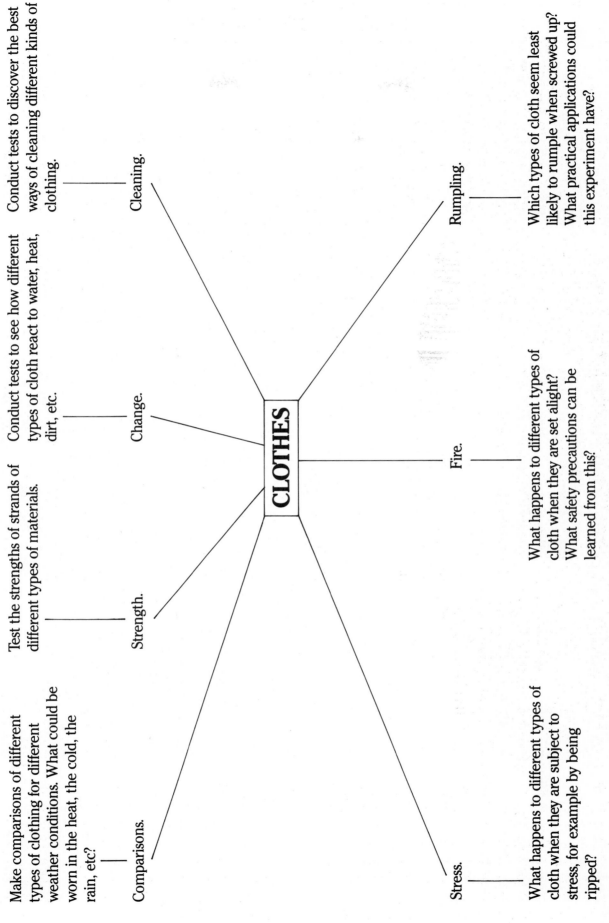

Make comparisons of different types of clothing for different weather conditions. What could be worn in the heat, the cold, the rain, etc?

Comparisons.

Test the strengths of strands of different types of materials.

Strength.

Conduct tests to see how different types of cloth react to water, heat, dirt, etc.

Change.

Conduct tests to discover the best ways of cleaning different kinds of clothing.

Cleaning.

CLOTHES

Which types of cloth seem least likely to rumple when screwed up? What practical applications could this experiment have?

Rumpling.

What happens to different types of cloth when they are set alight? What safety precautions can be learned from this?

Fire.

What happens to different types of cloth when they are subject to stress, for example by being ripped?

Stress.

Projects on materials: Bridges (AT4: Materials and their behaviour)

BRIDGES

Comparisons.

Make a study of different bridges in the area: beam, suspension and arch. Watch videos about bridges. Draw them and write about them.

Testing.

Make cardboard models of the three main types of bridge. Devise tests for effectiveness, strength, reliability.

Changes.

Make a study of the formation of rust on different metals. How could this affect the building and maintenance of a bridge?

Converting raw materials.

Make model bridges out of different materials – wood, stone, paper, cardboard, etc. Which materials are the strongest? Which are the easiest to build with? Which look best?

Reactions.

What kinds of wood make the best arch bridges? Experiment with many different kinds. Which of them bend and which do not?

What happens to different types of steel if they are left outside for a few months? What changes occur?

Make a model bridge out of cardboard. How does it react to different properties – water from a watering can, air from a jet, stones placed on it, etc?

Projects on materials: Bricks (AT4: Materials and their behaviour)

BRICKS

Comparisons.
Collect as many different types of brick as possible. Compare them. How do they differ? In what ways are they the same? What are their various functions? Are they interchangeable?

Absorption.
Place different bricks in a bucket of water for a few hours. Which absorb the most water? Which absorb the least water? How can this discovery affect the use of the bricks in building?

Change.
Leave a number of different bricks outside for a few months. How do they react and change after exposure to the elements?

Adding and separating.
What has to be mixed together to make mortar? Use the mortar to build a small wall.

Strength.
Which seems the strongest, a wall made of stones, or a wall made of bricks? What tests can you devise for this?

Reaction.
How do blocks of clay react to being baked in the oven? How do they react to being baked in the sun? What is the difference? Which way of making bricks seems the best? Why?

Properties.
Hammer a piece of brick into dust. How has the brick changed? Would it be possible to make some sort of brick out of the dust? How?

Projects on the Earth

The projects on the Earth given here are 'Air', 'Light and dark' and 'The Sun'.
● 'Air' examines air pollution, the ways in which air influences the weather, the sky and the different types of cloud, night and day, and space travel.
● 'Light and dark' looks at pollution, natural and artificial light, the effects of natural light on the growth of plants and animals, space, the stars, and the reflection of light.
● 'The Sun' considers the solar system, the energy the Sun produces, its effects on growth, and the drawbacks and dangers associated with the Sun.

Projects on the Earth: Air (AT3: Earth and environment)

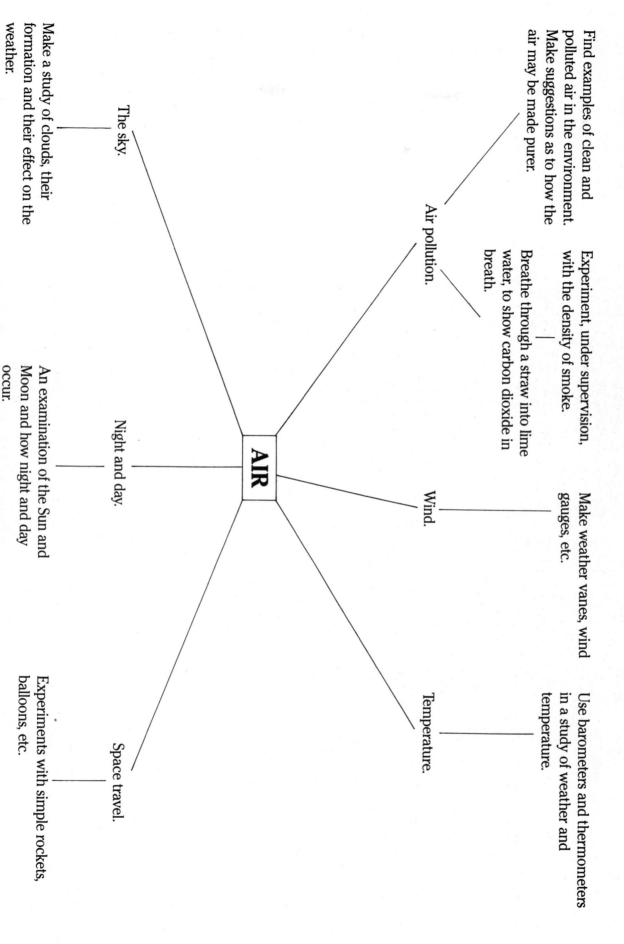

AIR

Air pollution.

Find examples of clean and polluted air in the environment. Make suggestions as to how the air may be made purer.

Experiment, under supervision, with the density of smoke.

Breathe through a straw into lime water, to show carbon dioxide in breath.

Wind.

Make weather vanes, wind gauges, etc.

Temperature.

Use barometers and thermometers in a study of weather and temperature.

Space travel.

Experiments with simple rockets, balloons, etc.

Night and day.

An examination of the Sun and Moon and how night and day occur.

The sky.

Make a study of clouds, their formation and their effect on the weather.

Projects on the Earth: Light and dark (AT3: Earth and environment)

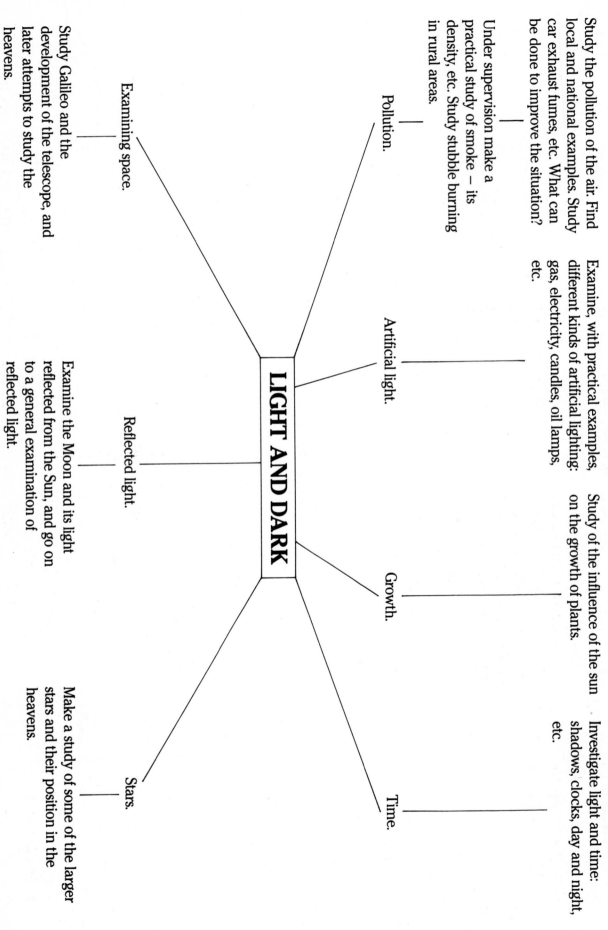

LIGHT AND DARK

Pollution.
Study the pollution of the air. Find local and national examples. Study car exhaust fumes, etc. What can be done to improve the situation?

Under supervision make a practical study of smoke — its density, etc. Study stubble burning in rural areas.

Artificial light.
Examine, with practical examples, different kinds of artificial lighting: gas, electricity, candles, oil lamps, etc.

Study of the influence of the sun on the growth of plants.

Growth.

Time.
Investigate light and time: shadows, clocks, day and night, etc.

Stars.
Make a study of some of the larger stars and their position in the heavens.

Reflected light.
Examine the Moon and its light reflected from the Sun, and go on to a general examination of reflected light.

Examining space.
Study Galileo and the development of the telescope, and later attempts to study the heavens.

138

Projects on the Earth: The Sun (AT3: Earth and environment)

The dangers of too much sun in some parts of the world – drought, poor soil, etc.

The importance of sunlight to plants and all growing things.

The sun above us.

The Moon circling the earth and giving off reflected light from the Sun.

Make a study and comparison of forms of artificial lighting and heating, including solar heating and electric light.

Examine the safety precautions needed when dealing with the sun – the dangers of looking directly at the sun, and of too much exposure to its rays. Discuss dealing with sunburn, and other first-aid measures.

The dangers of sunlight.

THE SUN

The solar system.

Earth and the other planets in the solar system.

Harnessing the energy of the Sun.

The place of the Sun as the centre of the solar system.

Projects on forces

The projects on forces suggested here are 'Transport', 'Wheels', 'Bells' and 'Torches'.
● 'Transport' looks at different ways of moving real and toy vehicles, and the effects of temperature and movement on people and on objects.
● 'Wheels' brings together work on gears, electricity as a source of movement, air pressure and the transfer of energy.

● 'Bells' considers bells in all their variety – from hand-bells, church bells, alarm clocks and buzzers to animal bells. The correlation between shape and pitch, or resonance, is considered, as is the use of electricity in making a buzzer work.
● 'Torches' is a study of electricity and magnetism, the transference of energy, and light and dark.

Projects on forces: Transport (AT5: Energy and its effects)

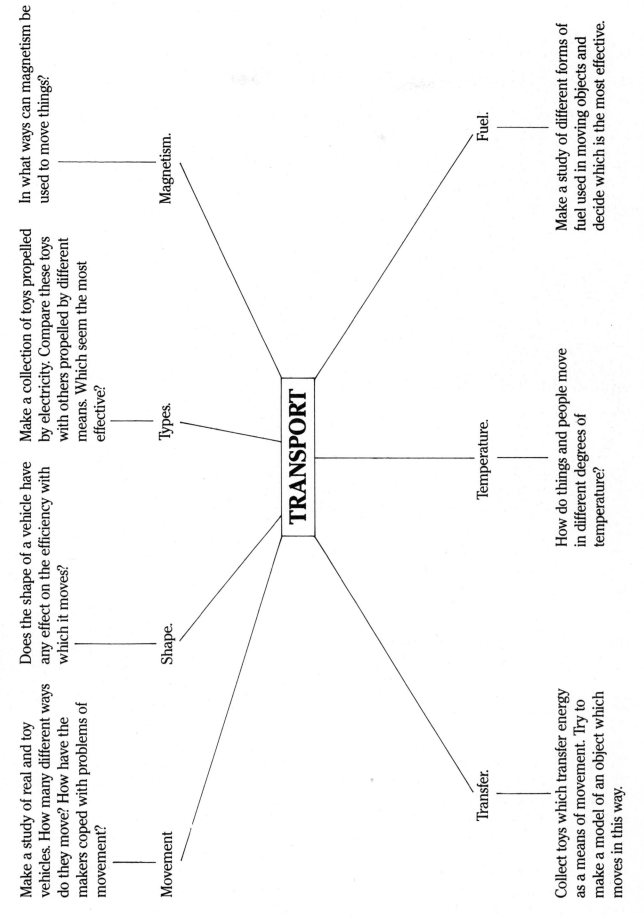

TRANSPORT

Magnetism.
In what ways can magnetism be used to move things?

Types.
Make a collection of toys propelled by electricity. Compare these toys with others propelled by different means. Which seem the most effective?

Shape.
Does the shape of a vehicle have any effect on the efficiency with which it moves?

Movement
Make a study of real and toy vehicles. How many different ways do they move? How have the makers coped with problems of movement?

Fuel.
Make a study of different forms of fuel used in moving objects and decide which is the most effective.

Temperature.
How do things and people move in different degrees of temperature?

Transfer.
Collect toys which transfer energy as a means of movement. Try to make a model of an object which moves in this way.

141

Projects on forces: Wheels (AT5: Energy and its effects)

WHEELS

Gears.

Make a study of gears and the ways in which they move wheels. Make two cog-wheels out of lollipop sticks and fit them into one another.

Hoops.

Roll a number of different-sized hoops across the playground. Which cover the ground most effectively? Does the size or weight of a hoop have a bearing on its efficiency?

Movement.

Can the children devise an electrical circuit which can move a small wheel?

Make a study of wheeled vehicles propelled by electricity. What are their advantages and disadvantages? Test electrically propelled toys.

Air pressure.

How does the air pressure in a bicycle wheel remain constant? What keeps the air in? How can the tyre be made firmer? Make a study of pumps and valves.

Cycling.

How is the energy from a cyclist transferred to the cycle, making it move?

Angles.

How much more energy is needed to ride a bicycle up a hill than on the flat? Why is this?

Projects on forces: Bells (AT5: Energy and its effects)

Make an electrical circuit which will sound a bell or a buzzer.

Circuits.

Instruments.

Ask the children to try to devise and make a hand-bell which will work.

Make a study of electric alarm clocks. How do they differ and how are they the same?

Alarm clocks.

Making music.

Can the children make music in teams, using hand-bells of different pitches?

If the clapper in a bell is changed in shape, by having cloth put over it or clay stuck to it, does it alter the pitch or the resonance of the bell?

Shape.

BELLS

Animal bells.

Devise a bell which will go around the neck of a cow or other animal, which will be operated by the movement of the animal.

Make a collection of hand-bells. How do they work? What sort of noise does each one make? Does the degree of force with which a bell is shaken make a difference to the strength of the noise?

Movement.

Church bells.

Try to find some church bells and study them. What forms of energy are used to make them work? How much energy has to be used up by the ringers when the bells are operated by hand?

143

Projects on forces: Torches (AT5: Energy and its effects)

TORCHES

Transference.

How is energy transferred in a torch? How does the 'on-off' switch operate?

Testing.

Take six identical torches and put in batteries of similar strength but different make. Turn on the torches. Which battery lasts the longest? Is this reflected in its price?

Messages.

Ask the children to devise a code to be used by flashing a torch to pass on messages.

Making a torch.

Ask the children to devise an electrical circuit which could be used as a torch. What sort of base will they need? Will their torch need protective covering and an aperture? Will they need a circuit breaker?

Light travels.

Show that light travels in a straight line by getting the children to look at the beams of torches in a darkened room.

Silhouettes.

Demonstrate the formation of shadows by using a torch to illuminate the heads of children while silhouettes are drawn.

Chapter Six
Cross-curricular projects

This chapter contains a wide range of ideas for cross-curricular projects on the themes of 'Rivers', 'Trees' and 'Farming', with particular relevance to Key Stage 2. These and similar projects can be used to deliver many aspects of the National Curriculum.

As in Chapter Three, which dealt with projects for Key Stage 1, particular emphasis has been given to the potential for science work within each project, but ideas have also been given for work within many other curricular areas.

Science

Pollution

Take some samples of water from different parts of a river and examine them for pollution. Make a number of filters out of pieces of blotting paper of the same type and size. Ask the children to pour the different samples of water through the filters into jars.

What changes occur in the water as it emerges from the filters? What is left in the filters? Let the children compare the samples of water. Which seems the cleanest, and which the dirtiest? How can they judge this? Can they think of any possible reason for the different levels of pollution in different areas of the river? Can the children devise other filters, using sand, pebbles, gravel and different types of cloth, and decide which is the most effective?

Erosion

Show the children how the action of a flowing river can cause erosion. Ask them to place some small pieces of chalk in a bottle of river water and shake it vigorously for some time. What happens to the chalk in the water? How does it change shape? How do parts of the chalk become almost dissolved in the water? Do some of the pieces sink to the bottom of the bottle? Does the colour or consistency of the water change?

Assuming that stones and rocks of all sorts receive similar treatment from a swiftly flowing river, what can the children deduce about the part played by rivers in the general process of erosion?

Pressure

Let the children make a model of hills out of papier mâché, and then create a river and a dam. The papier mâché model should be constructed over a base of crumpled wire netting moulded into the shape of hills and valleys, and tacked to a suitably-sized stout board about a metre square or larger. Put several layers of papier mâché, constructed

from small pieces of torn newspaper, over the netting. When the papier mâché has dried out thoroughly, paint it with emulsion paint and put a layer of polyurethane varnish on top. Construct hills all round the edges of the board to keep the water in. Pour water into the valleys. Let the children find a suitable narrow spot in the landscape to build a dam. Ask them to decide on the best material for a solid model, experimenting with stone, wood and Plasticine. What effect does the dam have on the landscape above the dam? What happens to the landscape below the dam? What would happen to the landscape in front of the dam if the dam were breached? Could water be allowed through one part of the dam in a controlled manner on to the land below, and, if so, what could the pressure of this water be used for? Could the force of this pressure be altered by the size of the hole bored in the dam?

Design and technology

Water wheels

Let the children design and build a water wheel to be powered by flowing water from a tap or a simulated river on the school field. They could make it from a cork with pieces of plastic stuck in it to act as the slats of the wheel, or they could make a more sophisticated model consisting of two cog-like wheels with a stick through the middle of the wheels to balance the whole thing over a river. What practical uses do the children think these wheels could be put to?

Mathematics

Measurement

Observing all safety precautions and under strict supervision, the children could measure the width and depth of suitable stretches of a river or stream. Ask them to work out how fast the water is flowing by timing the journey of a tennis ball over a measured stretch of the river. How long would it take the ball to travel twice as far, ten times as far, etc? Discover the rate of water evaporation on the river banks by pouring 50 ml of water into a dish and measuring and recording the weight-loss every hour. How can the children apply this finding to the whole river? Where does the evaporated water go?

Geography

Rivers of Great Britain

Make a study of the major rivers of Great Britain, especially the one nearest the school. Where does it start and where does it finish? What sort of shipping may be found on it? Are there locks, waterfalls, bridges or rapids in the area near the school? Does part of the river have to be dredged? Why is this? What fish are found in it, and what sort of wildlife and wildflowers occupy its banks?

History

The Vikings

Make a study of the Vikings' attacks on the east coast of England in the ninth century AD, and their forays up the rivers of this coast. In longships crewed by about forty warriors, the Scandinavians navigated by observing the position of the sun at midday and by the Pole Star at night. They ravaged the farms, villages and religious settlements of the coast, and sailed up the Trent and Humber rivers. There is a legend that the port of Grimsby, at the mouth of the river Humber, was founded by a fisherman called Grimm on the proceeds of the reward he received from a Viking king for sheltering the king's son.

Religious education

The Baptism of Jesus

Study the story and religious significance of John the Baptist's baptism of Jesus in the river Jordan at the outset of Jesus' ministry. Jesus wished to begin his work with a public act of submission to the will of God. Look at the significance of the different types of baptism within the Christian church.

English

Literature

Read *The Wind in the Willows* by Kenneth Grahame (Puffin) and *The River at Green Knowe* by Lucy Boston (Puffin).
Read the following poems:

The Pied Piper of Hamelin

Great rats, small rats, lean rats, brawny rats,
Brown rats, black rats, grey rats, tawny rats,
Grave old plodders, gay young friskers,
Fathers, mothers, uncles, cousins,
Cocking tails and pricking whiskers,
Families by tens and dozens,
Brothers, sisters, husbands, wives —
Followed the Piper for their lives.
From street to street he piped advancing,
And step for step they followed dancing,
Until they came to the river Weser,
Wherein all plunged and perished!

Robert Browning

The Lays of Ancient Rome

But meanwhile axe and lever
Have manfully been plied;
And now the bridge hangs tottering
Above the boiling tide.
"Come back, come back, Horatius!"
Loud cried the Fathers all.
"Back Lartius! back, Herminius!
Back, ere the ruin fall!"

Lord Macaulay

Talking

Ask the children to describe the crossing of the River Weser from the point of view of:
● the Pied Piper,
● a rat,
● someone going for a swim in the river at the time,
● a child doing a project on the pollution of the river water.

Writing

Encourage the children to write part of a television script about the defence of the bridge by Horatius and his companions.

Music

Singing

Sing the following songs with the children:
● 'One More River' (traditional)
● 'We Are Crossing Jordan River' (traditional)
● 'By The Waters of Babylon' (traditional).

Trees

Science

Buds
In the spring, go with the children to collect twigs with buds on them from as many different trees as possible. Put the twigs in vases of water. Ask the children to examine and record the growth of the buds, and see how long it takes for the different buds to develop. As the buds open, the new leaves should emerge. The children could make drawings of these. How many leaves come out of each bud? Does this number alter from species to species? Compare the different rates of growth of the buds growing on the twigs in water with those of the buds still on the trees. Which set of buds grows the quickest and strongest? What could cause this?

Tree life
Collect fallen leaves and tree debris from the foot of a tree. Put everything in a light-coloured bowl in a warm classroom. Ask the children to record the number and variety of minibeasts which emerge from the leaves and debris. Are there spiders among them? What other kinds of creatures are there? What do they live on, and why have they chosen the base of a tree as their home?

Measuring trees
Encourage the children to work out ways of measuring the height of a tree. Measure a child and ask her to stand at the foot of a tree. Can the children estimate the height of the tree, using the height of the child? How many times taller than the child does the tree seem to be?

Another method of doing this is to measure the child and ask her to stand against the tree as before. Then step back, holding a pencil at arm's length, until the pencil appears to cover the entire height of the tree. Mark on the pencil the level reached by the child's head. You can now calculate the tree's height based on your knowledge of the child's height. Ask the class to try this several times, with different children standing against the tree. Their calculations for the height of the tree should come out roughly the same each time.

Recycling paper
Paper is made from wood. It is possible to recycle paper and use it again. Experiment with making different types of paper. Ask the children to collect newspaper, blotting paper, tissue paper and so on. Then they can mash each type of paper to a pulp in water, and add some starch to rebind the mixture. Let them press the pulp into a thin layer on an absorbent surface and allow it to dry. Can they devise tests to see which type of recycled paper is the most effective?

Design and technology

Build a wooden shelter
Collect fallen branches and foliage from different trees. Let the children work in groups, each group using the branches of a different tree. Ask them to design and build an overnight shelter for one child. They should conduct tests to ensure that the shelter is reasonably stable, windproof and rainproof. Which type of tree seems to provide the best branches for such a shelter?

Mathematics

Branch spread
Ask the children to find out how widely the branches of a tree extend in different directions. They can use an ordinary magnetic compass to find north and a protractor to give the bearings in degrees. First they should put the compass on the ground at the base of the tree. They could use a long tape to measure along the ground from the trunk to the end of the longest branch in a northerly direction. Ask them to repeat this at ten-degree intervals, and then make a chart to show the different bearings and branch lengths.

Geography

The Amazon rainforests
Tropical rainforests are very dense. The trees are never bare, and the leaves are so close together that they blot out the sun. Rain falls almost every day. The sun heats the air and makes it rise, taking with it the moisture from the trees. As it rises, the air cools, and then comes down again as rain.

The Indian tribes of the South American rainforests are losing their homes as the trees are cut down for commercial purposes. Because the trees are being cut down, there are not so many of them to give off oxygen, and this is having a harmful effect on our planet. Ask the children to conduct an investigation to find out what is being done to prevent the cutting down of the rainforests.

History

Saxon homes
When the Saxons settled in Britain in the sixth century AD, the country was still densely forested. The Saxons tended to develop villages rather than live in towns. They often used oak for the main beams of the floor and walls of their houses, and ash and hazel wood for the roofs. The houses were probably thatched with straw or reeds.

Art

Bark rubbings
Ask the children to fasten a piece of thick paper to a trunk of a tree or a fallen piece of bark. Using cobbler's wax or large wax crayons, let them rub over the paper to make a picture.

English

Literature
Read *The Jungle Books* by Rudyard Kipling

(Macmillan) and *The Tree in the Moon* by Rosalind Kerven (Cambridge University Press). Read the following poems:

The Way Through the Woods
They shut the road through the woods
Seventy years ago.
Weather and rain have undone it again,
And now you would never know
There was once a road through the woods
Before they planted the trees.
It is underneath the coppice and heath,
And the thin anemones.

Rudyard Kipling

and

Throwing a Tree
The two executioners stalk along over the knolls,
Bearing two axes with heavy heads shining and wide,
And a long limp two-handed saw toothed for cutting great boles,
And so they approach the proud tree that bears the death-mark on its side.

Thomas Hardy

Talking
Encourage a class debate on the following subject: if there is an urgent need for timber for building, is there a case to be made for cutting down whole forests?

Writing
● Why do you think they shut the way through the woods in the poem *The Way Through the Woods?* Write a story telling why the road was closed.
● Imagine that you have heard that some trees are going to be cut down near you so that bungalows may be built. Write and perform a five-minute radio advertising campaign to alert people to what is happening and to rally them to the support of the trees.

Music

Singing
Sing the following songs:
● 'Lazy Coconut Tree' (Edwards/Coombes);
● 'The Wild Oak Tree' (traditional).

Farming

Science

Conditions needed for plant growth

Let the children conduct a controlled experiment to see what conditions are needed to grow plants. Take five small jars and put some blotting paper in each. Put some seeds in the jars. Set up different growing conditions in each jar. The first three jars could be placed in a warm, light environment, the fourth in a dark place and the fifth in a refrigerator. The conditions in each jar could be as follows:

Jar 1: Seeds on their own. Conditions: light, warmth, air, no water.

Jar 2: Seeds with a little water. Conditions: light, warmth, air and water.

Jar 3: Seeds with cooled boiled water (to remove air), with a few drops of oil on top (to stop air entering water). Conditions: light, warmth, water, no oxygen.

Jar 4: Seeds with a little water. Conditions: air, warmth, moisture, no light.

Jar 5: Seeds with a little water. Conditions: air, water, no light, no warmth.

Let the children examine the seeds after a week to see which are beginning to grow. Seeds need water, air and warmth; later they can make and store their own food. Does this experiment bear out the statement that only water, air and warmth are needed for seed germination?

Measuring the growth of plants

Let the children plant different seeds in pots indoors. They could put an acorn in one pot, a chestnut in another, a broad bean in another, and so on. Ask them to half-fill each pot with soil, plant the seed and then put more soil on top until the pot is almost full. They should water each pot and wait until the plant starts growing above the surface of the pot.

Ask them to measure the growth of each plant regularly and compare the different rates of growth.

Studying soil

Study a piece of waste land near the school. Dig a hole straight down and observe the changing colours of the soil. Ask the children to work out how far down the roots of nearby plants go. This usually marks the limit of the fertile topsoil. Dig holes in other areas and let the children measure the limits of the roots of the plants. Which area has the greatest depth of topsoil? How would the children use this information if they were thinking of farming one of the areas?

Design and technology

Seed spreader

Can the children devise and make a machine on wheels which will spread seeds evenly over a patch of freshly dug soil? What will they use to contain the seeds? How will they allow the seeds to drop evenly? How can the machine be pulled or pushed over the soil?

Mathematics

Estimating

Dig up a piece of land one metre square and ten centimetres deep. How many worms can the children find in this patch? How many worms would there be in a patch of five metres, ten metres and fifty metres, assuming that the same number of worms occupied each metre of soil?

Geography

Crops

Let the children make a study of the different kinds of crops grown by farmers.

Cereals are wheat, barley, oats and rye. Wheat is ground into flour, barley is used in the brewing of beer, oats are used for porridge and rye is mainly used for feeding animals.

Other forage crops grown for animal feed

include kale, rape, vetches and mustard. They may be eaten green or packed tightly into a mound. Grass may be used for forage or for the making of hay.

Root crops are good for the soil and may also be used for animal food; the main types are mangolds, turnips and swedes.

Other common crops include sugar beet, which is made into sugar, and pulses, which are peas and beans.

Ask the children to collect examples or pictures of each type of crop.

History

Iron Age farming

About 500 BC, the Celts in Britain began to smelt and temper iron and make farming implements from iron. They worked the soil which was easy to farm on the soft ground along rivers. On the hilltops they kept sheep and cattle. From hand-ploughs they developed a heavier, iron-tipped plough drawn by oxen. With this they could till the heavy, fertile lowland soil. They could also use iron axes to clear the trees from wooded areas. Fields became larger and farmers had a surplus of grain to sell.

Religious education

The parable of the sower

Discuss the meaning of the parable of the sower with the children:

'A sower went out to sow. And as he sowed, some seed fell along the footpath; and the birds came and ate it up. Some seed fell on rocky ground, where it had little soil, and it sprouted quickly because it had no depth of earth; but when the sun rose the young corn was scorched, and as it had no root it withered away. Some seed fell among thistles; and the thistles shot up, and choked the corn. And some of the seed fell into good soil, where it bore fruit, yielding a hundredfold, or, it might be, sixtyfold or thirtyfold'.

(Matthew 13, 4-9)

English

Literature

Read *Little House in the Big Woods* by Laura Ingalls Wilder (Methuen) and *The Hungry Snow* by Fay Sampson (Dobson).
Read the following poems:

Sheep in Winter

The sheep get up and make their many tracks,
And bear a load of snow upon their backs,
And gnaw the frozen turnip to the ground
With quick sharp bite, and then go noising round . . .

John Clare

The Banks of the Condamine

O, hark the dogs are barking, love,
I can no longer stay.
The men are all gone mustering
And it is nearly day.
And I must off by the morning light
Before the sun doth shine,
To meet the Sydney shearers
On the banks of the Condamine.

Anon

Talking

Ask the children to prepare and deliver a number of different weather forecasts in the manner of a television presenter. Each forecast must please a different person:
● A boy who does not want to go to school,
● An Australian sheep shearer,
● A wheat farmer.

Writing

● Let the children make up a modern parable with a modern farm as its background.
● Ask the children to write their own version of *The Banks of the Condamine*, as if they were sheep shearers who did *not* want to get up and meet the others by the river.

Music

Singing

Sing with the children 'Old Macdonald Had a Farm' (anon).

Chapter Seven
Assessment and recording

The matter of assessing and recording the work of children has probably caused more unease in the teaching profession than any other aspect of the National Curriculum. On the one hand there is a demand for a comprehensive system for charting the progress of each child, but on the other hand, many teachers are worried about the amount of time that such testing and reporting will take. A prudent horticulturist, after all, does not have to keep pulling up a plant by its roots to see how it is getting on.

However, assessment and recording are here to stay. As teachers we should endeavour to ensure that the system we adopt is both thorough and succinct.

In the primary school, standard assessment tasks are to be set at the end of Key Stages 1 and 2, at the ages of 7 and 11, in the core subjects of English, science and mathematics. These tests are intended to have three distinct purposes:
● To be formative; to develop and promote better teaching and learning,
● To be summative; to inform parents about their child's progress and to add to their information about the child and her education,
● To be aggregated; to provide a collected body of information for the wider public in order that judgements may be made about attainment in a school or local education authority.

Each school should devise its own method of assessment and recording, based on the needs of its children and teachers. Such a system should enable the teacher to check whether individual children in the class are working at the appropriate levels in each area of study. The information provided should be capable of being transmitted easily and plainly to parents, and should be used by other teachers when a child changes classes or schools.

The profile of a child which emerges from an appropriate system of assessment and subsequent recording should enable anyone studying it to see what general themes have been used, which attainment targets have been covered and what particular investigations the child has undertaken at specific levels.

Record sheets

Each child should have her own record sheet showing what she has accomplished. It is not enough to note what has been attempted; some provision must be made for showing what the child has grasped. In *National Curriculum and Assessment* (DES, July, 1990),

John MacGregor, Secretary of State for Education and Science, makes this point:

'Assessment is intrinsic to the National Curriculum. It is nothing less than the means by which we can all keep track of what pupils have *learned* – as distinct from what they have been *taught*. As such, it is a key part of the teacher's professional equipment. It is the means by which the teacher recognises the strengths and weaknesses of individual pupils, and is enabled to adapt his or her teaching to meet those needs so that strengths can be fostered and weaknesses tackled.'

Schools are requested to devise record sheets which suit their own needs. The model given here has three columns for the teacher to fill in after each activity. **Covered** means that the subject has been taught. **Grasped** means that in the opinion of the teacher, the child understands the particular point being made. **Revised** means that the teacher has returned to the subject at a later date. Depending upon the time available, each column could be completed with a tick or with the date upon which the subject was covered, grasped or revised.

Record sheets for
Key Stages 1 and 2, Levels 1 to 5

AT2: Life and living processes (types and needs of living things)

Levels	Activities	Covered	Grasped	Revised
1	● Examine wildlife in the environment. ● Study the growth of plants. ● Keep and study wildlife in the classroom.			
2	● Experiment with plants to understand that sunlight is essential to growth. ● Help look after wildlife in the classroom to grasp that living things need to be treated with care.			
3	● Study roots and stems to see similarities and differences in living things. ● Sort and classify seeds in different ways.			
4	● Study types of soil to examine the processes of decay. ● Collect fossils and understand that animals and plants may be preserved in this way. ● Conduct experiments with plants to understand that they need air and water, and that they benefit from fertilizers.			
5	● Study a spider and its web to grasp the concept of predator and prey.			

AT2: Life and living processes (organisation, survival and reproduction of living things)

Levels	Activities	Covered	Grasped	Revised
1	● Study objects in the environment to grasp the idea that some things are living, some dead, and some have never lived. ● Using charts and practical examination, name the main parts of the human body and of plants.			
2	● Study plants and creatures to grasp the concept that living things reproduce their own kind. ● Make a study of the importance of cleanliness and hygiene. ● Keep diaries of the pattern of the school day. ● Study the life-cycles of creatures.			
3	● Conduct experiments to study basic life processes involving the heart, lungs, stomach, etc.			
4	● Study flies and other creatures to examine reproduction in wildlife. ● Conduct studies with foodstuffs to understand the growth of microbes and the importance of hygiene. ● Make practical examinations of the major organs of flowering plants.			
5	● Study cells by looking at the skin of an onion under a microscope.			

AT2: Life and living processes (living things, extinct forms of life, genes)

Levels	Activities	Covered	Grasped	Revised
1	● Compare the physical abilities of children through a series of tests. ● Compare the differences between pets belonging to the children.			
2	● Compare the measurements of all children in the class.			
3	● Examine fossils, and construct time-charts to reinforce the concept of the past. ● Make model fossils from plaster of Paris.			
4	● Measure the differences between living organisms by comparing the children's physical strength.			
5	● Introduce the concept of genetic inheritance by comparing the children's eye and hair colour with that of their parents.			

AT2: Life and living processes (pollution, waste, recycling, human activity and change in the environment)

Levels	Activities	Covered	Grasped	Revised
1	● Take part in a project to keep the classroom clean. ● Study common objects and decide what waste products they may produce.			
2	● Observe worms in a glass case to see them passing soil through their bodies, thus breaking it up. ● Experiment with different materials to understand that waste products decay naturally over different periods.			
3	● Collect examples of polluted water, and clean it to show how it may be recycled.			
4	● Investigate how the school's litter is collected and disposed of. ● Recycle old jars, papers, clothes, etc.			
5	● Grow various types of moulds and study microbes. ● Compare objects and sort them according to whether they are biodegradable or non-biodegradable.			

AT3: Earth and environment (main natural features of Earth and atmosphere)

Levels	Activities	Covered	Grasped	Revised
1	• Collect and compare natural objects. • Study different weather conditions.			
2	• Make a study of seasonal changes. • Observe the effect of weather on people's lives. • Record weather conditions.			
3	• Conduct experiments to show that air is all around us. • Observe the weathering of rocks. • Investigate a natural material.			
4	• Study the wind by making wind gauges, etc. • Make a study of the effects of climate on agriculture.			
5	• Study rock stratas. • Study the water cycle.			

AT3: Earth and environment (the solar system, Moon, Sun, changes in the night sky)

Levels	Activities	Covered	Grasped	Revised
1	• Study a particular part of the environment at different seasons. • Investigate how we get day and night.			
2	• Show how the length of a day changes through a year. • Establish that the Sun, Moon and Earth are separate bodies.			
3	• Investigate the movement of the Earth.			
4	• Study the composition of the solar system. • Investigate the major groupings of stars.			
5	• Study the phases of the Moon.			

AT4: Materials and their behaviour (chemical reactions, uses, properties and change in materials)

Levels	Activities	Covered	Grasped	Revised
4	● Examine rusted objects in a study of chemical change. ● Observe chemical change in dissolving tablets. ● Convert raw materials into useful products.			
5	● Use raw materials by making bricks, kites, water wheels, etc. ● Study biochemical processes by dissolving different substances.			

AT4: Materials and their behaviour (developing the use of models to explain structure and properties of materials)

Levels	Activities	Covered	Grasped	Revised
4	● Study the constitution of matter by melting candle wax, etc. ● Study reactions by striking matches, etc.			
5	● Begin to consider atoms by powdering charcoal; understand that the smallest piece contains many molecules.			

AT4: Materials and their behaviour (textures, shapes, properties)

Levels	Activities	Covered	Grasped	Revised
1	• Study the shapes and materials of local buildings. • Examine wallpapers and other materials for texture.			
2	• Apply various stresses to different materials. • Group materials by their characteristics. • Demonstrate that heating and cooling may cause changes in materials.			
3	• Make model walls of different materials and devise tests for their strength. • Compare natural and manufactured materials. • Compare similarities and differences in everyday materials.			
4	• Investigate how bricks stand up to weather conditions and compare simple properties. • Make model bridges of different types and compare their strengths. • Show that liquids occupy volume by filling different-shaped containers with water. • Classify materials into solids, liquids and gases.			
5	• Show that gases have 'weight' by boiling a kettle and measuring the water before and after steam has appeared. • Separate mixtures such as sand and salt.			

AT5: Energy and its effects (pushing, pulling, floating, sinking, gravity, etc)

Levels	Activities	Covered	Grasped	Revised
1	• Use different forces on objects – pulling, pushing, lifting, etc.			
2	• Experiments with pushes and pulls on toys.			
3	• Experiment with floating and sinking. • Demonstrate forces by moving toys on ramps.			
4	• Experiment with stirring, using different forces. • Show the force of gravity by dropping objects. • Show that weight is a force: slow down moving objects by placing weights on them.			
5	• Investigate the strength of structures with model rafts, bridges, etc. • Demonstrate friction by pulling objects over various surfaces.			

AT5: Energy and its effects (food, fuel, heat and coolness, the storing and use of energy)

Levels	Activities	Covered	Grasped	Revised
1	• Test to find the best runners, jumpers, etc. • Conduct diet surveys.			
2	• Understand the concepts of hot and cold by deciding which are the hot and cold places in the school. • Demonstrate how energy may be stored and released by tightening elastic bands around pencils. • Devise experiments with levers.			
3	• Construct and use a home-made thermometer. • Use toys which transfer energy – bows, gears, etc.			
4	• Make a study of the foods eaten by the class. • Study heating and cooling and their effects.			
5	• Conduct an energy-saving campaign. • Study dwindling global resources.			

AT5: Energy and its effects (properties, transmission and absorption of sound)

Levels	Activities	Covered	Grasped	Revised
1	• Make a study of sounds in the environment.			
2	• Experiment with the distances travelled by sound. • Make a number of simple musical instruments. • Discover which objects muffle sound and which ones allow it to travel.			
3	• Study the vibration of sound. • Show how sound travels through different materials.			
4	• Use a starter's pistol to show that it takes time for sound to travel.			
5	• Experiment with different types of pitch. • Investigate the loudness of sound and the amount of vibration caused. • Study the importance of noise control.			

AT5: Energy and its effects (origins of light, colour, reflections, light and shadow)

Levels	Activities	Covered	Grasped	Revised
1	• Examine objects which give off their own light. • See how light comes from different sources. • Discriminate between and match colours. • Study colour in the environment.			
2	• Investigate how light passes through some materials but not others.			
3	• Show how light can change direction. • Conduct investigate mirrors and reflection.			
4	• Investigate how light travels quickly and in straight lines. • See how shadows are formed.			
5	• Use prisms to investigate the colours of sunlight.			

AT5: Energy and its effects (magnetism, electrical circuits)

Levels	Activities	Covered	Grasped	Revised
1	● Study the everyday use of electricity.			
2	● Make a practical study of magnetic and non-magnetic objects.			
3	● Construct a simple electrical circuit. ● Make a study of objects which conduct electricity and those which do not.			
4	● Experiment with different electrical circuits.			
5	● Vary the flow of electricity in a circuit by setting up and using a Morse code transmitter.			

Record sheets for Attainment Target 1

As this attainment target should run through the science curriculum, it could be recorded as a form of revision for the whole curriculum, using the charts on the following pages as record sheets.

AT1: Scientific investigation

The numbers across the top of the chart opposite correspond to the numbers in the key below. Use the chart to tick off aspects of AT1 which have been dealt with in other attainment targets.

Key
1　Observe at first hand.
2　Describe and communicate.
3　Ask questions.
4　Identify differences.
5　Use measures.
6　List and collate.
7　Interpret findings by association.
8　Record findings.
9　Formulate hypotheses.
10　Identify variables.
11　Distinguish between tests.
12　Select and use instruments.
13　Quantify variables.
14　Record experimental findings.
15　Interpret pictograms and bar charts.
16　Interpret observations generally.
17　Describe activities by sequencing major features.
18　Raise questions in a form which can be investigated.
19　Formulate testable hypotheses.
20　Construct 'fair tests'.
21　Plan investigations using variables.
22　Use measuring instruments.
23　Follow written instructions and diagrams.
24　Carry out investigations with regard to safety.
25　Record results by appropriate means.
26　Draw conclusions from experimental results.
27　Describe investigations using technical vocabulary.

AT1: Scientific investigation

AT	Level	1	2	3	4	5	6	7	8	9	10	11	12	13	14	15	16	17	18	19	20	21	22	23	24	25	26	27
2	1																											
	2																											
	3																											
	4																											
	5																											
3	1																											
	2																											
	3																											
	4																											
	5																											
4	1																											
	2																											
	3																											
	4																											
	5																											
5	1																											
	2																											
	3																											
	4																											
	5																											

Scientific aspects of information technology including microelectronics

The letters at the top of the chart are defined in the key below. Use the chart to keep track of the application of IT to the other attainment targets.

Key

A   Know about some everyday devices which receive text, sound or images over long distances, using IT.

B   Know that there are many ways of communicating information over long distances.

C   Know that information can be stored using a range of everyday devices, including a computer.

D   Be able to store informaton using devices such as tape recorders and digital watches.

E   Know that information can be stored electronically in a variety of ways involving text, numbers, pictures and sound.

F   Be able to retrieve and select text, numbers, sound or graphics stored on a computer.

G   Know about the range of microelectronic devises used in everyday life.

H   Be able to detect and measure environmental changes using a variety of instruments.

I   Understand the function of and be able to use switches and relays in simple circuits.

J   Understand logic gates and their use in decision making and simple control circuits.

AT	Level	A	B	C	D	E	F	G	H	I	J
2											
3											
4											
5											

Booklist

For children

Nelson Science series, Stephen Hopkins and Anne Hunter (Nelson).
Science Horizons series, Jim Hudson, Cyndi Milliband, and Derek Slack (Macmillan).
Think and Do series, Sue Dale Tunnicliffe (Blackwell).
The Young Scientist Investigates series, Terry Jennings (OUP).
Collins Primary Science series, Linda Howe (Collins).
Science 'Early Learner' Books series, Bob Graham (Blackie).
Active Science series, Albert James (Schofield and Sims).
Science from the Beginning series,

B L Hampson and K C Evans (Oliver and Boyd).
Sciencewise series, Sheila Parker and Alan Ward (Nelson).
Reading About Science series, ed. Stuart Kellington (Heinemann).
Science Happenings series, Michael Holt (Ginn).

For teachers

Developing Science in the Primary Classroom Wynne Harlen and Gordon Smith (Macmillan).
Health Education from 5-16 HMI (HMSO).
Environmental Education from 5-16 HMI (HMSO).
Planning Scientific Investigations at Age 11 APU (DES).

Appendix A

The application of Attainment Target 1: Scientific investigation

It would be impracticable and counter-productive to try to include every skill delineated in AT 1 in each science activity undertaken with a class. The teacher should endeavour to spread these skills across a whole series of activities, remembering that while not all of them can be used at any one time, several will be covered more than once within a topic. Most of the skills should come into use

naturally and automatically as the horizons of the child are expanded under the guidance of the teacher.

The following example looks at a project about bridges, which covers Attainment Target 4, Materials and their behaviour. It shows how Attainment Target 1 can form an integral part of the work.

Bridges

Activity	Aspects of AT 1 involved
Look at local bridges.	Observe at first hand.
Talk and write about them and draw them.	Describe and communicate.
Ask questions, read books and watch videos to find out what types of bridges they are.	Ask questions.
	Identify differences.
	List and collate.
	Identify variables.
Make cardboard models of the three main types of bridges.	Select and use instruments.
	Use measuring instruments.
	Use measures.
Devise ways of testing the effectiveness, strength and reliability of model bridges.	Formulate hypotheses.
	Distinguish between tests.
	Construct 'fair' tests.
	Record experimental findings.
Make a study of rust on different materials, including bridges.	Interpret observations generally.
	Plan investigations.
Make model bridges out of different materials and test for various qualities.	Describe activities by sequencing major features.
	Record results by appropriate means.
	Draw conclusions from experimental results.
	Describe investigations.

Appendix B

Integrating a health education policy into the science curriculum

The following activities and their relevant attainment targets show one way of integrating a health education policy into the science curriculum, using ATs 1, 2 and 5.

Level	Activity
1	Know how to look after pets and wildlife, and study their needs.
1	Investigate the use of parts of the body, the senses, etc.
1	Make a study of the food we eat.
1	Examine differences in the needs of wildlife.
1	Study and collect litter in school.
2	Study the habitat of wild creatures and see how they protect themselves.
2	Examine the conditions of growth for plants.
2	Study health and hygiene – diet, sleep, etc.
2	Make a study of exercise and the major organs.
2	Examine the ways in which animals adapt to their environment. How should we observe safety precautions in everyday life?
2	Study the importance of water in our lives.
3	Examine the response of wildlife to seasonal changes. How can we adapt to different forms of weather and climate?
3	Make a study of the basic life processes – breathing, feeding, etc.
3	Read about extinct wildlife. Why and in what ways did creatures fail to survive?
3	Take part in a project to help preserve the local environment.
4	Examine the processes of decay, and study bacteria and moulds.

Level	Activity
4	Know about the factors which contribute to good health and body maintenance, including hygiene, and the avoidance of drugs, tobacco and alcohol.
4	Measure variations in living organisms, comparing the physical abilities of different children.
4	Examine waste products and recycling.
5	Study predator-prey relationships; this could be related to road safety.
5	Examine nutrition and healthy eating.
5	Study the passing on of information in the form of genes.
5	Describe various forms of pollution, and consider ways of preventing them.

Appendix C

Integrating a sex education policy into the science curriculum

A sex education policy can be pursued within the science curriculum through the following activities, using ATs 1, 2 and 5.

Level	Activity
1	Study a wide variety of living things, including humans.
1	Learn the names of external parts of the human body and of plants.
1	Know that human beings vary from one individual to the next.
1	Study the groupings of living things — family life.
2	Understand how living things are looked after and that they need care and consideration.
2	Know that living things reproduce their own kind.
2	Know that living things grow, change, grow old and die.
2	Measure simple differences between children.

Level	Activity
3	Make a study of change, including change in our bodies.
3	Know that basic life process are common to all living things, but that there are different lifestyles within communities and among living things in general.
3	Make a study of the main stages in the human life cycle.
3	Know that some life-forms are extinct, but that new life is constantly coming into being.
4	Study the reproduction of plants and animals.
4	Understand that after death plants and animals can be preserved as fossils.
4	Study the health and upbringing of babies.
4	Understand the process of reproduction in mammals.
4	Describe the main stages of flowering plant reproduction.
4	Be able to measure variations in living organisms.
5	Study different species in relation to their environment. How do they breed and look after their young?
5	In a study of predator-prey relationships, understand the importance of the family for mutual protection, consolation and love.
5	Study human procreation and birth.
5	Be able to describe the functions of the major organ systems, including the reproductive ones.
5	Know that information in the form of genes is passed on from one generation to the next.

Other Scholastic books

Bright Ideas

The Bright Ideas books provide a wealth of resources for busy primary school teachers. There are now more than 20 titles published, providing clearly explained and illustrated ideas on topics ranging from *Word Games* and *Science* to *Display* and *Classroom Management*. Each book contains material which can be photocopied for use in the classroom.

Bright Ideas for Early Years

The *Bright Ideas for Early Years* series has been written specially for nursery and reception teachers, playgroup leaders and all those who work with 3- to 6-year-olds. The books provide sound practical advice on all areas of learning. The ideas and activities are easy to follow and clearly illustrated.

Teacher Handbooks

The Teacher Handbooks give an overview of the latest research in primary education, and show how it can be put into practice in the classroom. Covering all the core areas of the curriculum, the *Teacher Handbooks* are indispensable to the new teacher as a source of information and useful to the experienced teacher as a quick reference guide.

Management Books

The Management Books are designed to help teachers to organise their time, classroom and teaching more efficiently. The books deal with topical issues, such as *Parents and Schools* and organising and planning *Project Teaching*, and are written by authors with lots of practical advice and experiences to share.

Let's Investigate

Let's Investigate is an exciting range of photocopiable activity books giving open-ended investigative tasks. Designed to cover the 6- to 12-year-old age range these books are ideal for small group or individual work. Each book presents progressively more difficult concepts and many of the activities can be adapted for use throughout the primary school. Detailed teacher's notes outlining the objectives of each photocopiable sheet and suggesting follow-up activities have been included.